Helen in Egypt

ALSO BY H. D.

Hermetic Definition

Trilogy

Helen in Egypt

by H.D.

Introduction by Horace Gregory

A NEW DIRECTIONS BOOK

Copyright © 1961 by Norman Holmes Pearson
Introduction copyright © 1961 by Horace Gregory

Manufactured in the United States of America
First published by Grove Press in 1961
Published clothbound and as New Directions Paperbook 380 in 1974
Published simultaneously in Canada by McClelland & Stewart, Ltd.

Library of Congress Cataloging in Publication Data

Doolittle, Hilda, 1886–1961.
    Helen in Egypt.

    (A New Directions Book)
    Poem.
    1. Helen of Troy—Poetry. I. H. D. II. D., H.
III. Title.
PS3507.O726H37 1974   811'.5'2   74–8563
ISBN 0–8112–0543–6
ISBN 0–8112–0544–4 (pbk.)

New Directions Books are published for James Laughlin
by New Directions Publishing Corporation
333 Sixth Avenue, New York 10014

Contents

Introduction

Who is Helen in Egypt? The argument at the very beginning of the poem indicates her origin:

We all know the story of Helen of Troy but few of us have followed her to Egypt. How did she get there? Stesichorus of Sicily in his Pallinode *was the first to tell us. . . . According to the* Pallinode, *Helen was never in Troy. She had been transposed or translated into Egypt. Helen of Troy was a phantom, substituted for the real Helen. . . . The Greeks and the Trojans alike fought for an illusion.*

And who was Stesichorus of Sicily? He was a Greek lyric poet (*ca.* 640–555 B.C.) a contemporary of Sappho and Alcaeus, and whose pen name, "Stesichorus," means Choir-setter. He was the inventor of the choral heroic hymn, and in that form raised lyric verse to the stature of the epic. He probably inspired Euripides to write his *Helen* in which, as the first scene shows us, Helen is in Egypt. All this is, of course, post-Homeric, yet post-Homeric versions of a myth often owe their inspiration to earlier, to half-forgotten, pre-Homeric sources. The only survival of Stesichorus' twenty-six books of poems is a fragment of fifty lines. H.D.'s *Helen in Egypt* is no translation, but a re-creation in her own terms of the Helen-Achilles myth.

Today it is believed that the fall of Troy took place about 1200 B.C. (As any historian knows, ancient dates shift according to theories in the measurement of time.)

In a like scale of measurement, the Homeric epics came three hundred years later. By 900 B.C. the fall of Troy, as well as the complex of tragedy, both Greek and Trojan, surrounding it — due to Greek genius — had become timeless. In the fall of Troy was its beginning. It possessed the imagination of the poets. Troy's end became the center of a galaxy of myths, a cycle in which the present tense is in a continual process of becoming (which is the language of poetry), in which the past becomes the future. It is appropriate that the overlying theme of H.D.'s *Helen in Egypt* is one of rebirth and resurrection.

In her re-creation of the Helen-Achilles myth, it is no less appropriate that H.D. has chosen to wear the mask of Stesichorus. Her poem is written in a series of three-line choral stanzas; it is a semidramatic lyric narrative; each change of scene, each change of voice is introduced by a brief interlude in prose. Far from distracting the eye and ear of the reader, the design of the poem sustains the flow of its variations, and preserves its narrative unity. This innovation in the writing of *Helen in Egypt* is characteristic of H.D.'s art, for from the day that Ezra Pound presented her early poems as examples of "Imagiste verse" she has been known as one of the principle innovators in American poetry. Although she has frequently acknowledged that the years of her early training in the writing of poetry owe their debts to Pound's remarks in his "A Few Don'ts for Imagistes," her lyric gifts soon transcended the limitations of a school of writing. Since 1931, the publication date of her book of poems, *Red Roses for Bronze*, it has been a misnomer to define her poems as

"Imagiste verse." "However," she said, "I don't know that labels matter very much. One writes the kind of poetry one likes. Other people put labels on it. Imagism was something that was important for poets learning their craft early in this century. But after learning his craft, the poet will find his true direction." Without denying the brilliance of Pound's remarks in "A Few Don'ts for Imagistes," it is true that the poets of that early group (all were young and high spirited) who later achieved distinction did so because of the individual merits of their poetry. Only those who pay more attention to labels than to poetry itself are likely to become confused by talk of "movements" and "poetic manifestoes." It is clear that the memorable poets (including H.D. and Pound himself) among the "Imagistes" were *not* confused. These were the innovators of poetic form, and not those who wrote for the sake of merely seeming "new" or experimental.

H.D.'s concern has been centered upon the nature of reality, or as she has said less abstractly, more modestly, "a wish to make real to myself what is most real." Her innovations are allied to that concern, to evoke the timeless moment in a brief lyrical movement and imagery of verse. In the creation of her style no living poet has exerted a greater discipline in the economy of words. This is one of the reasons why H.D. is so often regarded as a "poets' poet," the creator of a classic style in modern verse. Her adaptation of Euripides' *Ion* is less known than her shorter lyrics, nor are her longer poems in *The Walls Do Not Fall*, *Tribute to the Angels*, and *The Flowering*

of the Rod, written in London during World War II, as
well known as they should be. In retrospect these have
become the forerunners of *Helen in Egypt*, the preparation
for writing a new kind of lyric narrative, one in which the
arguments in prose act as a release from the scenes of
highly emotional temper in the lyrical passages.

The scenes of *Helen in Egypt* may be accepted as visions
perceived after the event of the Trojan War. The war
years of the Greek and Trojan ancients were no less vivid,
less total in their results than our half-century of wars to-
day. Without mentioning parallels between them, the
situations in *Helen in Egypt* contain timeless references to
our own times. It is as though the poem were infused with
the action and memory of an ancient past that exist
within the mutations of the present tense. It is H.D.'s
achievement to make us *feel* their presence. The dramatic
scenes in the poem are written in defense of "hated
Helen" — and the conflicts of Helen's guilt are the
springs of tension throughout the poem. The scenes are
also a showing forth, an epiphany of the cycle of myths
surrounding the active images of Achilles and Helen,
visions in memory of her relationship to Thetis, strange
scenes between Helen and Achilles, as well as those which
show her meetings with Theseus and Paris — but I shall
not attempt to paraphrase the poem. As every intelligent
reader of poetry knows, to paraphrase a poem is an im-
possibility, nor is it possible to reiterate in prose the actual
meanings contained within the poem. During the past
thirty years there have been many attempts to give
T.S.Eliot's *The Waste Land* various meanings. These suc-

ceeded only in bewildering the author — and he was left the choices of being amused, or flattered, or annoyed. It is best to say that *Helen in Egypt* increases its spell at each rereading. A line of the poem reads, "the old enchantment holds"— and that is true. Through the intonations of its choral music, the poem is an enchantment: there is magic in it.

The twentieth century is not without its singular re-creations of Greek myths. Of these Joyce's *Ulysses* is best known. No less singular is André Gide's essay in monologue, his *Theseus*. One can neither compare nor contrast H.D.'s *Helen in Egypt* with these. They are works in prose. Her poem is not an epic; it borrows nothing from the essay or the novel; yet like the other two books, it stands alone. It is a rarity.

In twentieth-century poetry, book-length poems of the first order are also rare, and H.D.'s *Helen in Egypt* is among them. The classic spirit that inspires and sustains a poem of this length is almost lost: *Helen in Egypt* is a sign of its recovery.

— Horace Gregory

PALLINODE

Book One

[1]

We all know the story of Helen of Troy but few of us have fol-
lowed her to Egypt. How did she get there? Stesichorus of Sicily
in his Pallinode, *was the first to tell us. Some centuries later,*
Euripides repeats the story. Stesichorus was said to have been
struck blind because of his invective against Helen, but later was
restored to sight, when he reinstated her in his Pallinode. *Eurip-*
ides, notably in The Trojan Women, *reviles her, but he also*
is "restored to sight." The later, little understood Helen in
Egypt, *is again a* Pallinode, *a defence, explanation or apology.*

According to the Pallinode, *Helen was never in Troy. She*
had been transposed or translated from Greece into Egypt. Helen
of Troy was a phantom, substituted for the real Helen, by jealous
deities. The Greeks and the Trojans alike fought for an illusion.

Do not despair, the hosts
surging beneath the Walls,
(no more than I) are ghosts;

do not bewail the Fall,
the scene is empty and I am alone,
yet in this Amen-temple,

I

I hear their voices,
there is no veil between us,
only space and leisure

and long corridors of lotus-bud
furled on the pillars,
and the lotus-flower unfurled,

with reed of the papyrus;
Amen (or Zeus we call him)
brought me here;

fear nothing of the future or the past,
He, God, will guide you,
bring you to this place,

as he brought me, his daughter,
twin-sister of twin-brothers
and Clytaemnestra, shadow of us all;

the old enchantment holds,
here there is peace
for Helena, Helen hated of all Greece.

Lethe, as we all know, is the river of forgetfulness for the shadows, passing from life to death. But Helen, mysteriously transposed to Egypt, does not want to forget. She is both phantom and reality.

The potion is not poison,
it is not Lethe and forgetfulness
but everlasting memory,

the glory and the beauty of the ships,
the wave that bore them onward
and the shock of hidden shoal,

the peril of the rocks,
the weary fall of sail,
the rope drawn taut,

the breathing and breath-taking
climb and fall, mountain and valley
challenging, the coast

drawn near, drawn far,
the helmsman's bitter oath
to see the goal receding

in the night; everlasting, everlasting
nothingness and lethargy of waiting;
O Helen, Helen, Daemon that thou art,

we will be done forever
with this charm, this evil philtre,
this curse of Aphrodite;

so they fought, forgetting women,
hero to hero, sworn brother and lover,
and cursing Helen through eternity.

*Her concern is with the past, with the anathema or curse. But
to the Greeks who perished on the long voyage out, or who died
imprecating her, beneath the Walls, she says, "you are forgiven."
They did not understand what she herself can only dimly appre-
hend. She may perceive the truth, but how explain it? Is it possible
that it all happened, the ruin — it would seem not only of Troy,
but of the "holocaust of the Greeks," of which she speaks later —
in order that two souls or two soul-mates should meet? It almost
seems so.*

Alas, my brothers,
Helen did not walk
upon the ramparts,

she whom you cursed
was but the phantom and the shadow thrown
of a reflection;

you are forgiven for I know my own,
and God for his own purpose
wills it so, that I

stricken, forsaken draw to me,
through magic greater than the trial of arms,
your own invincible, unchallenged Sire,

5

Lord of your legions, King of Myrmidons,
unconquerable, a mountain and a grave,
Achilles;

few were the words we said,
nor knew each other,
nor asked, are you Spirit?

are you sister? are you brother?
are you alive?
are you dead?

the harpers will sing forever
of how Achilles met Helen
among the shades,

but we were not, we are not shadows;
as we walk, heel and sole
leave our sandal-prints in the sand,

though the wounded heel treads lightly
and more lightly follow,
the purple sandals.

Had they met before? Perhaps. Achilles was one of the princely suitors for her hand, at the court of her earthly father, Tyndareus of Sparta. But this Helen is not to be recognized by earthly splendour nor this Achilles by accoutrements of valour. It is the lost legions that have conditioned their encounter, and "the sea-enchantment in his eyes."

How did we know each other?
was it the sea-enchantment in his eyes
of Thetis, his sea-mother?

what was the token given?
I was alone, bereft,
and wore no zone, no crown,

and he was shipwrecked,
drifting without chart,
famished and tempest-driven

the fury of the tempest in his eyes,
the bane of battle
and the legions lost;

for that was victory
and Troy-gates broken
in memory of the Body,

wounded, stricken,
the insult of the charioteer,
the chariot furiously driven,

the Furies' taunt?
take heart Achilles, for you may not die,
immortal and invincible;

though the Achilles-heel treads lightly,
still I feel the tightening muscles,
the taut sinews quiver,

as if I, Helen, had withdrawn
from the bruised and swollen flesh,
the arrow from its wound.

The Myrmidons are Achaeans in Thessaly, and by Achaei, *Homer designates the Greeks in general. But these legendary or archaic Greeks of the north are reputedly fair-haired, a race destined later to migrate and give the warrior-cult to Sparta. Here, values are reversed, a mortal after death may have immortality conferred upon him. But Achilles in life, in legend, is already immortal — in life, he is invincible, the hero-god. What is left for him after death? The Achilles-heel.*

This was the token, his mortality;
immortality and victory
were dissolved;

I am no more immortal,
I am man among the millions,
no hero-god among the Myrmidons;

some said a bowman from the Walls
let fly the dart, some said it was Apollo,
but I, Helena, know it was Love's arrow;

the body honoured
by the Grecian host
was but an iron casement,

9

it was God's plan
to melt the icy fortress of the soul,
and free the man;

God's plan is other than the priests disclose;
I did not know why
(in dream or in trance)

God had summoned me hither,
until I saw the dim outline
grown clearer,

as the new Mortal,
shedding his glory,
limped slowly across the sand.

The great Amen, Ammon or Amŭn temple still stands, so we may wander there with Helen. She and we need peace and time to reconstruct the legend. Karnak? Luxor? Thebes, certainly. This is the oldest city in the world. Homer knew it. But we look back, not so far geographically and historically. They had met on the coast in the dark. Achilles has been here with her; no doubt, he will come again. But for the moment, she wants to assess her treasure, realize the transcendental in material terms. For their meeting in eternity was timeless, but in time it was short, and "few were the words we said."

How did we greet each other?
here in this Amen-temple,
I have all-time to remember;

he comes, he goes;
I do not know that memory calls him,
or what Spirit-master

summons him to release
(as God released him)
the imprisoned, the lost;

few were the words we said,
but the words are graven on stone,
minted on gold, stamped upon lead;

they are coins of a treasure
or the graded weights
of barter and measure;

"I am a woman of pleasure,"
I spoke ironically into the night,
for he had built me a fire,

he, Achilles, piling brushwood,
finding an old flint in his pouch,
"I thought I had lost that";

few were the words we said,
"I am shipwrecked, I am lost,"
turning to view the stars,

swaying as before the mast,
"the season is different,
we are far from — from—"

let him forget,
Amen, All-father,
let him forget.

*Helen achieves the difficult task of translating a symbol in time,
into timeless-time or hieroglyph or ancient Egyptian time. She
knows the script, she says, but we judge that this is intuitive or
emotional knowledge, rather than intellectual. In any case, a night-
bird swooped toward them, in their first encounter on the beach.
To Achilles, lately arrived from Troy and the carnage of battle,
this is a "carrion creature," but Helen would banish these memories. She says she is "instructed," she is enchanted, rather. For
from the depth of her racial inheritance, she invokes (as the per-
ceptive visitor to Egypt must always do) the symbol or the "letter"
that represents or recalls the protective mother-goddess. This is no
death-symbol but a life-symbol, it is Isis or her Greek counter-
part, Thetis, the mother of Achilles.*

We huddled over the fire,
was there ever such a brazier?
a night-bird hooted past,

he started, "a curious flight,
a carrion creature — what—"
(dear God, let him forget);

I said, "there is mystery in this place,
I am instructed, I know the script,
the shape of this bird is a letter,

they call it the hieroglyph;
strive not, it is dedicate
to the goddess here, she is Isis";

"Isis," he said, "or Thetis," I said,
recalling, remembering, invoking
his sea-mother;

flame, I prayed, *flame forget,*
forgive and forget the other,
let my heart be filled with peace,

let me love him, as Thetis, his mother,
for I knew him, I saw in his eyes
the sea-enchantment, but he

knew not yet, Helen of Sparta,
knew not Helen of Troy,
knew not Helena, hated of Greece.

She is afraid, too. So she needs this protection. She has tried to conceal her identity with mockery, "I am a woman of pleasure." She knows what the Greeks think of her, and here is Greece-incarnate, the hero-god; true, he is shipwrecked; nevertheless, though wounded, he carries with him the threat of autocracy. She has lost caste. He is still Achilles. Or who is she? She says that Helen upon the ramparts was a phantom. Then, what is this Helen? Are they both ghosts? And if she is convinced of this, why does she entreat the flame that Achilles kindled, "let me love him, as Thetis, his mother"? Is she afraid of losing even her phantom integrity? And what of it? Thetis — Isis — Aphrodite — it was not her fault.

O—no—but through eternity, she will be blamed for this and she feels it coming. She will blacken her face like the prophetic femme noire *of antiquity. But it does not work. Achilles is here to impeach her. Why? We must blame someone. Hecate—a witch —a vulture, and finally, as if he had run out of common invective, he taunts her — a* hieroglyph. *This is almost funny, she must stop him, he is after all, the son of the sea-goddess. She has named Isis, the Egyptian Aphrodite, the primal cause of all the madness. But another, born-of-the-sea, is nearer, his own mother. Again, she thinks of her and reminds Achilles of his divine origin, "O child of Thetis." This is quite enough. Can you throttle a phantom? He tries. The end is inevitable.*

15

How could I hide my eyes?
how could I veil my face?
with ash or charcoal from the embers?

I drew out a blackened stick,
but he snatched it,
he flung it back,

"what sort of enchantment is this?
what art will you wield with a fagot?
are you Hecate? are you a witch?

a vulture, a hieroglyph,
the sign or the name of a goddess?
what sort of goddess is this?

where are we? who are you?
where is this desolate coast?
who am I?   am I a ghost?"

"you are living, O child of Thetis,
as you never lived before,"
then he caught at my wrist,

"Helena, cursed of Greece,
I have seen you upon the ramparts,
no art is beneath your power,

you stole the chosen, the flower
of all-time, of all-history,
my children, my legions;

for you were the ships burnt,
O cursèd, O envious Isis,
you — you — a vulture, a hieroglyph";

"Zeus be my witness," I said,
"it was he, Amen dreamed of all this
phantasmagoria of Troy,

it was dream and a phantasy";
O Thetis, O sea-mother,
I prayed, as he clutched my throat

with his fingers' remorseless steel,
let me go out, let me forget,
let me be lost . . . .

O Thetis, O sea-mother, I prayed under his cloak,
let me remember, let me remember,
forever, this Star in the night.

Book Two

[1]

But Helen seems concerned not only with the mystery of their
reconciliation but with the problem of why he had, in the first in-
stance, attacked her. There seems this latent hostility; with her
love, there is fear, yet there is strength, too, and defiance not only
of Achilles, but of the whole powerful war-faction.

Perhaps he was right
to call me Hecate and a witch;
I do not care for separate

might and grandeur,
I do not want to hear of Agamemnon
and the Trojan Walls,

I do not want to recall
shield, helmet, greaves,
though he wore them,

for that, I might recall them,
being part of his first
unforgettable anger;

I do not want to forget his anger,
not only because it brought Helen
to sleep in his arms,

but because he was, in any case,
defeated; if he strangled her
and flung her to the vultures,

still, he had lost
and they had lost —
the war-Lords of Greece.

But this host of Spirits, the Greek heroes? Without the Trojan War, she would never have found them or they would never have found her. Nor, we may presume, would she and Achilles have met in this out-of-time dimension. But Helen seems divided in her loyalties. She speaks of the "burning ember," the funeral pyre of the Greek heroes, and in her thought, dismisses Achilles, but we feel that she is really concerned with that other "burning ember . . . the flint, the spark of his anger."

It is the burning ember
that I remember,
heart of the fire,

consuming the Greek heroes;
it is the funeral pyre;
it is incense from the incense-trees,

wafted here through the columns;
never, never do I forget the host,
the chosen, the flower

of all-time, of all-history;
it was they who struck,
as the flint, the spark

of his anger, "no art is beneath your power";
what power drew them to me?
a hieroglyph, repeated endlessly,

upon the walls, the pillars,
the thousand-petalled lily;
they are not many, but one,

enfolded in sleep,
as the furled lotus-bud,
or with great wings unfurled,

sailing in ecstasy,
the western sea,
climbing sea-mountains,

dividing the deep valleys of the sea;
but now, go, go,
Achilles from me;

I feel the lure of the invisible,
I am happier here alone
in this great temple,

with this great temple's
indecipherable heiroglyph;
I have "read" the lily,

I can not "read" the hare, the chick, the bee,
I would study and decipher
the indecipherable Amen-script.

[3]

We were right. Helen herself denies an actual intellectual knowledge of the temple-symbols. But she is nearer to them than the instructed scribe; for her, the secret of the stone-writing is repeated in natural or human symbols. She herself is the writing.

I said, I was instructed in the writ;
but I had only heard of it,
when our priests decried

papyrus fragments,
travellers brought back,
as crude, primeval lettering;

I had only seen a tattered scroll's
dark tracing of a caravel
with a great sun's outline,

but inked-in, as with shadow;
it seemed a shadow-sun,
the boat, a picture of a toy;

I was not interested,
I was not instructed,
nor guessed the inner sense of the heiratic,

but when the bird swooped past,
that first evening,
I seemed to know the writing,

as if God made the picture
and matched it
with a living hieroglyph;

how did I know the vulture?
why did I invoke the mother?
why was he seized with terror?

in the dark, I must have looked
an inked-in shadow; but with his anger,
that ember, I became

what his accusation made me,
Isis, forever with that Child,
the Hawk Horus.

4

*Helen is a Greek, a Spartan, born from a sea-faring people.
Although in Egypt, it is not the primitive caravel, as she calls the
shadow or death-ship of Osiris, that she visualizes, when she
would recall the host of Spirits. Her vision is wholly Greek, though
she returns to the sacred Egyptian lily for her final inspiration.*

This is the spread of wings,
whether the Straits claimed them
or the Cyclades,

whether they floundered on the Pontic seas
or ran aground before the Hellespont,
whether they shouted Victory at the gate,

whether the bowmen shot them from the Walls,
whether they crowded surging through the breach,
or died of fever on the smitten plain,

whether they rallied and came home again,
in the worn hulks, half-rotted from the salt
or sun-warped on the beach,

whether they scattered or in companies,
or three or two sought the old ways of home,
whether they wandered as Odysseus did,

24

encountering new adventure, they are one;
no, I was not instructed, but I "read" the script,
I read the writing when he seized my throat,

this was his anger,
they were mine, not his,
the unnumbered host;

mine, all the ships,
mine, all the thousand petals of the rose,
mine, all the lily-petals,

mine, the great spread of wings,
the thousand sails,
the thousand feathered darts

that sped them home,
mine, the one dart in the Achilles-heel,
the thousand-and-one, mine.

5

But Helen returns to the caravel, the death-ship, as a suitable attribute of Osiris, "King and Magician, ruler of the dead." She senses the parallel. Has her knowledge made her happier? Perhaps. In any case, if Achilles has taunted her with her resemblance to Isis, and related the Isis-magic to a Hecate or witch-cult, so she sees clearly the duality of the legendary héros fatal.

The inked-in sun
within the caravel,
was symbol of Osiris,

King and Magician,
ruler of the dead,
and he was torn asunder

by his brother,
so they said,
the Whirlwind, Typhon;

so with the whirlwind
of the chariot-wheels,
the clang of metal

and the glint of steel,
Achilles lorded Simois plain,
as Typhon, the Destroyer;

destroyer and destroyed,
his very self was lost,
himself defeated;

the scattered host
(limbs torn asunder)
was the Osiris,

"the flower of all-time,
of all-history,
my children, my legions";

he lived, the immortal son
of the sea-goddess,
but anger made him sterner,

anger enclosed Osiris
within the iron-casement
of the Whirlwind, War;

they were not two but one,
Typhon-Osiris
to the initiate.

6

As Isis seeks to reclaim Osiris with the help of their Child, the sun-god Horus, so Helen, with the aid of "the unnumbered host" (symbolized by "the Hawk with the fiery pinions" or "the thousand-petalled lily") would gain spiritual recognition and ascendency over "Typhon, the Destroyer."

O Child, must it be forever,
that your father destroys you,
that you may find your father?

O Child, must the golden-feather
be forever forged by the Spirit,
released in the fury of war?

O Child, must you seek your mother
while your father forever
attacks her in jealousy,

"I begot them in death, they are mine";
must death rule life?
must the lily fade in the dark?

is it only the true immortals
who partake of mortality?
who but Helen of Troy

and Achilles, shipwrecked and lost,
dare claim you and know the Sun,
hidden behind the sun of our visible day?

does he speak of this?
does he acknowledge the thousand-petalled lily
that claimed its own,

the Hawk with the fiery pinions?
does he say, Helen,
you brought them to me?

not he — he comes, he goes —
back to the darkness?
called by a Spirit-master

to drive out the darkness,
to free the imprisoned,
even as God set him free?

7

But if she accuses Achilles of weighing "a feather's weight with a feather," she herself seems equally introspective. She seems to doubt her power, or the magic of the goddess Isis (Aphrodite, Thetis). She is jealous of "man, alone," the flight from laughter to the trumpet's call. She seems to doubt her power to lure Achilles from this, or the power of women in general. There is no good in this postulate. She will get nowhere. She knows this.

Will he forever weigh
Helen against the lost,
a feather's weight with a feather?

does he dare remember
the unreality of war,
in this enchanted place?

his fortress and his tower
and his throne
were built for man, alone;

no echo or soft whisper
in those halls,
no iridescent sheen,

no iris-flower,
no sweep of strings,
no answering laughter,

but the trumpet's call;
does he still wait the dead,
to challenge the celestial hierarchy?

whose are the dead
and whose the victory?
the light grows dim,

the riddle of the written stone
suddenly weighs me down;
why do I doubt, why wonder?

8

So being Helen of Troy, whether or not she ever walked upon the ramparts, she flings knowledge away. Let the temple walls flower with "the indecipherable Amen-script." It is not necessary to "read" the riddle. The pattern in itself is sufficient and it is beautiful.

Is Fate inexorable?
does Zeus decree that, forever,
Love should be born of War?

O Eros of flaming wings,
O Horus of golden feathers,
let my heart be filled with peace,

let me draw him back to this place;
alone, does he pace the beach,
does he question the wandering stars,

swaying as before the mast,
"the season is different,
we are far from — from —"

what heart-break, what unappeasable
ache, burning within his sinews,
as he remembers the arrow

32

that stole Immortality
and made him a Mortal;
let Helen's imperious quest

through this temple, to solve the riddle
written upon the Walls,
be shed, as a priestess' mantle;

no priestess calls him to me,
I ask not, nor care to know
what is or is not the answer,

whether as Orpheus he dared the depth of hell,
whether as Phaethon challenged the car of the sun,
whether he stole, as Prometheus stole

forbidden knowledge from heaven,
whether he broke the law,
(forgive me, O Zeus, the law-giver),

whether he changed, as Circe changed,
men into swine;
whether he flouted his power,

while women fell, as the scythe
of his visored glance swept them over;
whether he laughed as they fell;

whether he found, here and there,
a girl for a change in pleasure,
when weary after the fray

his elect slept in their tents;
whether here and there he stole a child,
here and there, everywhere,

luring youth into battle;
whether he cheated, he lied —
(he was brave? an immortal

to challenge mortality?) —
whether he razed a city,
a woman, or wore a crown

unearned by his merit —
he drew as a magnet drew
the ore from the rock?

gold from dross?
death from life?
was War inevitable?

Amen-Zeus, let me not ask,
but claim him and know the Sun,
hidden behind the sun of our visible day.

Book Three

[1]

Now they are both here in the temple, but Helen does not like the fixed stare of Achilles. This is not the "sea-enchantment in his eyes." She mistrusts this metallic glitter. He is thinking of the Battle. She speaks of the Greek islands in order to recall him, but, apparently, he is unmoved for she would dismiss him, "go, follow the ways of the sea." But he speaks her name, Helena, *and seemingly not altogether in character, asks an enigmatic question.*

I say, "what island shall we seek,"
to keep him from staring out
between the painted stele,

"shall it be Cos or Crete?"
I would rather forget,
I would rather forget,

but a phantom pursues him;
shall a phantom threaten my peace?
what does it matter,

who won, who lost?
must the Battle be fought and fought
in his memory?

and do I care,
do I care greatly
to keep him eternally?

I was happier alone,
why did I call him to me?
must I forever look back?

must I summon the names of home,
an enchantment to hold him here?
"shall we seek Cyprus' rose

or Naxos' purple grape?"
O do not turn, do not turn,
go, follow the ways of the sea;

but he turns, he speaks to me,
"Helena, which was the dream,
which was the veil of Cytheraea?"

2

*What does he mean? She does not know. We do not know. But
for the second time, he has spoken her name. That is sufficient. He
asks her of Cytheraea. She has been trying to charm him with the
names of Greek islands, but his charm or enchantment is stronger.
So strong that she must fight for her identity, for* Helena. *And
more than that, she must invoke or recall the "spread of wings." It
was "the thousand sails" that brought them together. If she forgets that, she is lost.*

What does he mean by that?
must I summon Hellenic thought
to counter an argument?

must we argue over again,
the reason that brought us here?
was the Fall of Troy the reason?

can one weigh the thousand ships
against one kiss in the night?
Helena?   who is she?

this was only the second time
that he uttered the deathless name,
for deathless it must remain;

I must fight for Helena,
lest the lure of his sea-eyes
endanger my memory

37

of the thousand-and-one darts;
it was they, the Holocaust,
a host, a cloud or a veil

who encircled, who sheltered me,
when his fingers closed on my throat;
much has happened

since that first night
on the desolate beach,
many the problems solved,

the answers given
by the Writing, the Amen-script,
but I started, as out of a trance,

to hear him speak my name,
and I was there again,
(was there ever such a brazier?)

I drew out a blackened stick,
to darken my arms,
to disguise my features,

but I could not hide my eyes;
he flung back the stick on the fire,
"are you Hecate? are you a witch?"

3

Achilles attacked her, certainly. But Helen returns again and again to "that first night on the desolate beach." We may surmise that this "attack" meant more to her than the approaches of her husband, Menelaus, or the seduction of her lover, Paris. (Provided of course, that Helen had ever been lured from Sparta to Troy.) And though Helen speaks of the "invisible host surrounding and helping me," she can also ask, "can one weigh the thousand ships against one kiss in the night?"

Much has happened
in timeless-time,
here in the Amen-temple,

but he had not questioned me,
he had never spoken of Beauty;
the rasp of a severed wheel

seemed to ring in the dark,
the spark of a sword on a shield,
the whirr of an arrow,

the crack of a broken lance,
then laughter mingled with fury,
as host encountered host;

39

but that had never been;
how long did he hesitate
in time or in timeless-time,

while his fingers tightened their grip?
why did he let me go?
did he hear the whirr of wings,

did he feel the invisible host
surrounding and helping me?
was he afraid of the dead?

[4]

*"One kiss in the night?" That is obviously, the dream. Helen
could have told him that. Instead, she defends herself with the
thought of her twin-brothers and "Eros, the Hawk Horus."*

Why should I answer him?
it was Zeus who summoned me here,
twin-sister of twin-brothers;

were they there, the Dioscuri?
was it they who brought the host
to witness the deathless glory

of the youth he had sent to death?
I say, a cloud in the night,
a swarm, encircled me,

must I tell him again their name,
the one name for the thousand lost,
Eros, the Hawk Horus?

41

"Which was the dream?" Surely, "the deathless spark of Helena's wakening."

So they swooped to their prey;
there was never such a spread of wings,
such a play of golden feathers,

though I did not see them,
I heard them, as I heard myself say,
O Thetis, O sea-mother;

let me forget the other,
for to-day is to-day,
ringed and rayed with the word "beautiful";

how shall I answer him?
what is the answer to
Helena, which was the dream?

the rasp of a severed wheel,
the fury of steel upon steel,
the spark from a sword on a shield?

or the deathless spark
of Helena's wakening . . .
a touch in the dark?

Helen says, "I am awake, no trance, though I move as one in a dream." But again she must reassure herself. She had said of herself and Achilles in Egypt, "we were not, we are not shadows" and she had insisted that "the hosts surging beneath the Walls, (no more than I) are ghosts." They are not shadows, not shades, not ghosts. What are they?

Yet never forgetful,
never unmindful of the Child,
Aphrodite sent,

Love begotten of War
and the sea-enchantment together;
the veil of Cytheraea?

a cloud or a swirl of snow,
a swarm, an infinite number,
yet one whole, one cluster of bees,

as a trail or a Galaxy
of numberless stars,
that seem one but are many;

it was they, the veil
that concealed yet revealed,
that reconciled him to me,

War and the sea-enchantment;
I am awake, no trance,
though I move as one in a dream.

7

Is the "veil of Cytheraea" or of Love, Death? Is the disguise of Death or the "veil" of Death, Love? This is too difficult a question to answer. Helen only knows that without the souls or "the sails of the thousand ships," her encounter with Achilles would have "burnt out in a flash" or burnt her out, like Semele, when Zeus at her request, "revealed himself." The dream? The veil? She does understand. But there must be an intermediate dimension or plane. She asks, "are we home-sick for what has been?"

The harpers will sing forever
of the unveiled Aphrodite,
a portent, an apparition;

but without the Galaxy,
the sails of the thousand ships,
the Glory that compassed me

when I faced his anger,
we would have burnt out in a flash,
as Semele when Zeus

revealed himself; her request
to confront God openly,
was answered by Death:

45

was Death the answer?
the Hawk with the thousand pinions,
the thousand-and-one darts?

the rise and fall of the sea,
the veil of Cytheraea?
are we home-sick for what has been?

I place my hand on a pillar
and run my hand as the blind,
along the invisible curve

or the line of chick or bee;
where are we?
and what is the answer?

8

*But still Helen wants "some simple answer." She feels that
Achilles can give it to her. But she delays asking the direct question that will tell her everything. When she introduces it, it is in a
roundabout way. She knows that her name was Helen, in Sparta,
in Greece. But she wants to know of that other, "walking upon
the ramparts." She does not directly ask Achilles if he recognizes
in her the Helen of his first accusation, "I have seen you upon the
ramparts." Is this Helen actually that Helen? Achilles seems
grudgingly to apologize for his first boorishness, "I was afraid."
Who indeed would not be, at sudden encounter with the admitted
first-cause "of all-time, of all-history." Fate, Death, Reintegra-
tion, Resurrection? What was she then, if she was there, at all, in
Troy? His answer is unequivocal and final, "a fountain of water
in that desert . . . we died of thirst."*

"Were you rapt in prayer?"
"no, Achilles, I wanted some simple answer
to your question";

"my question?"
"which was the dream";
"I asked you which was the veil;

the sea-roads lie between
you and the answer";
"you called me Helena";

47

"that was your name";
"*was* my name?"
"in Sparta, in Greece";

"and walking upon the ramparts?"
"I can see you still, a mist
or a fountain of water

in that desert; we died of thirst";
"but you never spoke my name
till you called me —"

"hist — enough —
I was afraid of evil,
in an evil place."

Book Four

[1]

So at last we see, with the eyes of Achilles, Helen upon the Walls.

Achilles: You say, I could not see,
               but God had given to me,
               the eyes of an eagle;

               you say, I could not know
               how many paces there were
               from turret to turret;

               there was bitter discussion and hate,
               she could leave by a secret gate,
               and the armies be saved;

               why does she hold us here?
               the winters were ruthless and bleak,
               the summer burnt up the plain

               and the army with fever;
               they fell as the ears of wheat
               when a reaper harvests the grain;

is this the harvest?
year after year, we fought
to enter a prison, a fortress;

was she a prisoner?
did she wanton, awake?
or asleep, did she dream of home?

an arrow would settle it,
but no man dared aim at the mark
that taunted and angered us;

and we asked, would an arrow pierce
a Daemon's heart? a devil?
had she enchanted us

with a dream of daring, of peril,
as yet un-writ in the scrolls of history,
un-sung as yet by the poets?

This is the Achilles of legend, Lord of the Myrmidons, indisputable dictator with his select body-guard, the seven, of whom he, the eighth, received the directives of campaign. Technically, he shares the Command, as he calls it, with Helen's discredited husband, Menelaus and with Agamemnon, the husband of her sister. There is also, Odysseus, with whom we gather, there has been some plot or compromise. Achilles will compromise for once, though this is not his usual way of fighting. There is evidently a bribe, some counter-bargaining. Agamemnon and Menelaus are too slow, too heavy-handed. Perhaps the plan of the wooden-horse, or the iron-horse, as he calls it, does not materialize before Achilles falls before the Scaean Gate. But there is some secret agreement. If Odysseus succeeds in his designs, Achilles will be given Helen and world-leadership. This is contrary to the first agreement of the allies.

I had broken the proud
and re-moulded them to my whim;
the elect, asleep in their tents,

were my slaves, my servants;
we were an iron-ring, unbreakable,
they shared immortality with Achilles,

the seven who could not die
while I directed the car of fire,
I, the eighth of the hierarchy;

into the ring of our Immortality,
there came with a clamour of arms,
as a roar of chargers, answering the trumpeter,

the Command; no swerving, no wavering,
proceed to the iron-gate,
to the gate of brass,

let Odysseus unfold his plan
of the iron-horse,
listen and make an end

of this tedious parleying;
approach, with all subtlety,
the Trojan House with a gift:

the Towers will fall;
Helen will be your share
of the spoils of war;

what is a promise given?
this is the iron-ring,
no Grecian or other king

may contest or disobey;
within the iron-circle of your fame,
no more invisible,

you shall control the world. . . .
how did the story end?
another took command.

[3]

He still seems to be arguing the point. It is evidently not in character for him to take second place. His Myrmidons have been first always. He must have some direct guidance. Where will he get it? He seems for once, to be at odds with the Command. "Did the Command read backward?" He will consult a new oracle; after all, it is only a "game of prophecy." He will watch Helen, measure her paces, the direction she takes, how and where she looks. If she pauses here or there — yes. If she goes on there or here — no. He forgets the vulnerability of the Achilles-heel and "Another took command."

I counted the fall of her feet
from turret to turret;
will the count even yesterday's?

will there be five over?
this was a game I played,
a game of prophecy;

if she turns and shields her eyes,
gazing over the plain —yes—;
if she waits as she waited

day before yesterday,
for ten heart-beats
before the second gate —no—;

what was the question
to which she gave the answer
with the measured fall of her feet,

or her pause over the rampart
that bridged the iron-gate?
shall we strike as my legions had struck,

first through the long fight,
or shall we take second place
and leave the Trojan's fate to Odysseus?

did the Command read backward?
I stooped to fasten a greave
that was loose at the ankle,

when she turned; I stood
indifferent to the rasp of metal,
and her eyes met mine;

you say, I could not see her eyes
across the field of battle,
I could not see their light

shimmering as light on the changeable sea?
all things would change but never
the glance she exchanged with me.

4

The symbolic "veil" to which Achilles had enigmatically re-
ferred now resolves itself down to the memory of a woman's scarf,
blowing in the winter-wind, one day before he had begun to tire of
or distrust the original oracle of the purely masculine "iron-ring
whom Death made stronger." Does he blame Helen for luring him
from the Command, which had evidently instructed him to follow
Odysseus?

We were an iron-ring
whom Death made stronger,
but when the arrow pierced my heel,

they were not there;
where were they? where was I
and where was Troy?

I seemed to know the whole,
but as a story told long ago,
forgotten and re-told;

the Walls fell
but it was a small matter,
and Odysseus' wanderings

that had not yet happened,
had happened long ago;
only the salt air and a gull hovering

seemed real, and an old sailor
who greeted me as a lost stranger,
resting his gnarled hands

on the oars, *where would you go?*
I did not know,
I saw her scarf

as the wind caught it,
one winter day; I saw her hand
through the transparent folds,

and her wrist and her throat;
but that was long ago,
in the beginning,

before I began to count
and measure her foot-fall
from turret to turret;

if I remember the veil,
I remember the Power
that swayed Achilles;

what had happened?
was the Command
a lure to destruction?

5

Is his reluctance to follow Odysseus or in any case "to take second place," even at the Command's suggestion, the cause of his death? His after-life apparently, was not what he expected. Where was the circle of immortals to hail and acclaim him? Time values have altered, present is past, past is future. The whole heroic sequence is over, forgotten, re-lived, forgotten again. Only one thing is certain, the caravel, as Helen had first called the death-ship of Osiris. And as on his first meeting with her, there are still "the familiar stars."

I do not remember
where or how I embarked,
only the sound of the rowlocks

as the old man ferried me out;
he made for a strange ship
that he called a caravel;

if I had thought at all,
I would have thought
of a caravel as a small boat,

but this had a mast;
swaying across the night,
I counted the flaming host

of the familiar stars,
the Bear and Orion's belt,
the Dragon, the glittering Chair;

the mast measured them out,
picture by picture,
the outline of hero and beast

grew clearer and clearer;
their names were Greek —
but a caravel?

I puzzled . . .
I found myself alone,
where had the crew gone?

6

Now Achilles himself admits defeat. For what had he lost "the rule of the world and Greece"? For two things, "the turn of a Greek wrist" and "a ship's mast that measured the stars."

I only remember the turn
of a Greek wrist,
knotting a scarf;

I only remember
the sway of a ship's mast,
that measured the stars;

I only remember
a struggle to free
my feet from a tangle of cords,

and a leap in the dark;
I only remember
the shells, whiter than bone

on the ledge of a desolate beach;
I only remember
a broken strap

that had lost Achilles
the rule of the world and Greece;
I only remember

how I had questioned Command;
for this weakness, this wavering,
I was shot like an underling,

like the least servant,
following the last luggage-carts
and the burdened beasts.

7

*The Command or the adamant rule of the inner circle of the
warrior caste was "bequest from the past." Equally, each group or
circle had its responsibility to the future. Had Achilles broken the
connection of "the present to aeons to come"? Was this the punish-
ment for his "game of prophecy"? Has he "lost in a game of
chance"?*

The Command was bequest from the past,
from father to son,
the Command bound past to the present

and the present to aeons to come,
the Command was my father, my brother,
my lover, my God;

it was not the Command that betrayed,
it was Another;
She is stronger than God, they say,

She is stronger than Fate
and a chaffing greave,
loose at the ankle,

but is She stronger, I asked,
stronger than Hercules?
for I felt Herculean strength

61

return when I saw Her face;
I remembered my Power
and the world that I had lost;

was it a trivial thing
to have bartered the world
for a glance?

but I had not bartered or bargained,
I had lost
in a game of chance.

8

It seems so. Achilles himself might be thought to lose stature by apology. Can he apologize? Or does he bargain, in a sense, play for time? Superficially now, they appear to accept second-best. Actually, they are both occupied with the thought of reconstruction, he "to re-claim the coast with the Pharos, the light-house," she to establish or re-establish the ancient Mysteries.

No— I spoke evil words,
forget them, repeat them not;
only answer my question,

how are Helen in Egypt
and Helen upon the ramparts,
together yet separate?

how have the paths met?
how have the circles crossed?
how phrase or how frame the problem?

I, too, question and wonder
though I am not rapt apart
as you in this Amen-temple,

and I am seldom here;
while I work to re-claim the coast
with the Pharos, the light-house,

ask the oracle to declare,
Helena, which was the dream,
which was the veil of Cytheraea.

Book Five

[1]

"How have the paths met?" This is indeed the lesser personal mystery. "The harpers will sing forever of how Achilles met Helen among the shades," but perhaps they can not tell us why they met, for exactly what reason "the circles crossed." This is part of the Greater Mystery. Helen will not force an answer from the oracle. She will take her time about it.

No, I will not challenge
the ancient Mystery,
the Oracle; I will walk

with measured step
the length of the Porch,
I will turn and walk back;

I will count the tread of my feet,
as a dancer counts,
faster or slower,

but never changing the beat,
the rhythm; I will go
from pillar to pillar,

from stele to pillar;
and round again to the river;
here, there are iron-rings

where the boats, in ancient times,
made fast, but the Nile
has changed its course;

only the temple-lake
contains the holy water;
it is enough; it was long ago

that the ships swayed here by the wharf;
it is stone and heavily built;
it was built to last forever.

2

*But in the meantime, she goes on examining the "pictures";
there is the boat again, a symbol of the death-ship that had brought
Achilles to her. There is the death-dealing dragon or Typhon-
serpent, "reared to attack," Achilles and herself, "crowned with
the helm of defence." Mutually, they would have destroyed each
other, but for "the wisdom of Thoth."*

So the pictures will never fade,
while one neophyte is left
to wonder again at the boat,

to relate the graven line
to a fact, graven in memory;
so in the Book of Thoth,

the serpent, reared to attack,
is Achilles' spring in the dark;
so the Goddess with vulture-helmet

is myself defenceless,
yet crowned with the helm of defence;
he had lost and I had lost utterly,

but for the wisdom of Thoth;
Amen-Thoth held the balance
as it swayed, till it steadied itself

with the weight of feather with feather;
it was Fate, it was Destiny,
as a magnet draws ore from a rock.

3

We are back now with our first meeting of Helen, in the Great Temple, when she says, "Amen (or Zeus we call him) brought me here." So recalling this Father, she remembers as on that first occasion, her "twin-brothers and Clytaemnestra, shadow of us all." It is as if Helen wanted to recall her immediate "family," as protection or balance against the overwhelming fact of her Fate or Destiny, this meeting with Achilles.

I am not happy without her,
Clytaemnestra, my sister;
as I turn by the last pillar,

I find Isis with Nephthys,
the Child's other mother;
the two are inseparable

as substance and shadow,
as shadow and substance are;
is she Nemesis or Astarte,

or Nepenthe, forgetfulness?
I would change my place for hers,
wherever she is, O Father,

why should Helen be given
peace through eternity,
and Clytaemnestra doomed,

and slain by her son, Orestes?
or is it a story told,
a shadow of a shadow,

has it ever happened,
or is it yet to come?
do I myself invent

this tale of my sister's fate?
Hermione, my child,
and Iphigenia, her child, are one.

4

She re-tells a story that may still be in the future, as Achilles
remembers "Odysseus' wanderings that had not yet happened."
Actually, Pylades did not marry Iphigenia, but Electra, the older
sister of Orestes.

I do not know when or whether
in time or in timeless-time
Orestes married my daughter;

was it before his flight
from the Furies, or after,
when he returned to life,

re-claimed at Athene's altar;
I do not know when or whether
Pylades and Iphigenia

were bound with the bridal wreaths;
but these re-tell the story,
repeat the picture

of Clytaemnestra and Helen,
Agamemnon and Menelaus;
but they are at one, not lost,

half, part of the tale of Troy,
half, bound to the Dioscuri;
twin-sisters of twin-brothers,

half of our life was given
to another hierarchy;
our children were children

of the Lords of the world and Troy,
but our birthright bound us to another dynasty,
other than Trojans and Greeks.

5

Why does Helen recall Iphigenia? Does she identify herself with her sister's child? Does she feel that she, like Iphigenia, was "a pledge to Death" and that like Iphigenia, she had been rescued at the last moment? She reminds us that Iphigenia was summoned to Aulis, on the pretext of a marriage to Achilles.

I will call my sister Nepenthe,
forgetfulness of the past,
remembrance of childhood together;

what did she care for the trumpet,
the herald's cry at the gate,
war is over;

it is true she lay with her lover,
but she could never forget
the glint of steel at the throat

of her child on the altar;
Artemis snatched away
the proffered sacrifice,

but not even Artemis could veil
that terrible moment,
could make Clytaemnestra forget

the lure, the deception, the lie
that had brought her to Aulis;
"we will pledge, forsooth, our dearest child

to the greatest hero in Greece;
bring her here
to join hand with hand

in the bridal pledge at the altar";
but the pledge was a pledge to Death,
to War and the armies of Greece.

By identifying Clytaemnestra with Iphigenia, "as one before the altar," it seems as if Helen were trying to re-instate her or dismiss her tragic story. It is as if Helen were re-living her own story and visualizing her own fate in terms of that of her twin-sister. Helen has been so signally favoured. She would recall Clytaemnestra and "remembrance of childhood together."

She was a bride, my sister,
with a bride's innocence,
she was a lover of flowers

and she wound in her hair,
the same simple weeds
that Iphigenia wore;

she stepped forward,
they stood together
as one, before the altar;

O Word of the Goddess,
O Harmony and Grace,
it was a moment

of infinite beauty,
but a war-Lord
blighted that peace.

74

*Does Helen feel that it was her sister's consummation in-time
that had led to disaster? Is she contrasting her sister's husband,
"her first lover," with her own? Does she possibly feel that her
desertion of Menelaus is comparable to her sister's murder of
Agamemnon? Do they share Nemesis together?*

Her last lover was nothing,
only support and stay
through the long days;

she was glad
when she drew the glaive
from the heart of her first lover;

she was glad when her son
stayed his hand,
to hear herself say,

remember Iphigenia;
she was glad to get away;
but where is she,

my sister, Nepenthe?
where is Nemesis?
where is Astarte?

75

*Helen compares Clytaemnestra and Iphigenia to "one swan and
one cygnet." Their divinity is stronger than all the material forces
gathered against them. They must forget the war and its conse-
quences — but no, there is this yet, unresolved — without war,
there would have been no Achilles, no "Star in the night."*

Have you ever seen a swan,
when you threaten its nest —
two swans, but she was alone,

who was never alone;
the wings of an angry swan
can compass the earth,

can drive the demons
back to Tartarus,
can measure heaven in their span;

one swan and one cygnet
were stronger than all the host,
assembled upon the slopes

and the hills of Aulis;
she was born of a Swan,
and I and our brothers,

76

we are children of Zeus;
I must wait, I must wonder again
at the fate that has brought me here;

surely, she must forget,
she must forget the past,
and I must forget Achilles . . .

———————————

. . . but never the ember
born of his strange attack,
never his anger,

never the fire,
never the brazier,
never the Star in the night.

Book Six

Initiation? Does Helen brush aside all the traditional philos-
ophy and wisdom, to imply that enlightenment comes or does not
come, as a gift, a whim "of this ancient Child, Egypt," rather
than as formal reward for recognized achievement?

You may ask why I speak of Thoth-Amen,
of Amen-Zeus or Zeus separately,
you may think I invoke or recall

a series of multiple gods,
a Lion, a Hawk or an Ibis,
as we were taught to think

of the child-like fantasy
of this ancient Child, Egypt;
how can you understand

what few may acknowledge and live,
what many acknowledge and die?
He is One, yet the many

manifest separately; He may manifest
as a jackal and hound you to death?
or is He changeable like air,

and like air, invisible?
God is beyond the manifest?
He is ether and limitless space?

you may ask forever, you may penetrate
every shrine, an initiate,
and remain unenlightened at last.

2

She again recalls the Greek scene. For it is through her Greek identity that she understands. She has accepted what she does not understand, "this ancient Child, Egypt." But she would gradually, it would seem, bring Egypt and Greece together. There is the treachery of Agamemnon, the betrayal of Clytaemnestra, of Iphigenia. These, from another world, still seem to claim her. Why? Obviously, because Achilles was involved somehow.

You will not understand
what I have taken years
or centuries to experience;

you may have a thousand loves
and not one Lover;
you may win a thousand wars

and not one Victory;
so I see further into the past,
into the future;

Achilles was the false bridegroom,
Achilles was the hero promised
to my sister's child,

promised to her,
promised to me,
promised to Iphigenia;

it was Achilles who stood by the altar
and did not interfere
with the treacherous plan,

the plot, they said, of Odysseus;
it was Agamemnon who commanded
her mother to bring her to Aulis,

but it was Achilles, Achilles
who sanctioned the sacrifice,
the gift of his bride to Death.

3

"God does not weave a loose web," no. Perhaps it is the beauty and proportion of the pattern that amazes Helen. It is not "in the oracles of Greece or the hieroglyphs of Egypt" that she finds the answer. It is in the simple remembrance of her first meeting with Achilles, and his recognition of her.

Artemis brought her to Tauris,
where her brother Orestes
with his friend Pylades, found her;

but there was another marriage,
as yet unconsummate;
God does not weave a loose web,

nor do his Daughters, the Fates;
it was years, it was centuries,
it was a fleeting moment,

but the Balance waited
the inevitable weight
of feather with feather;

how can you find the answer
in the oracles of Greece
or the hieroglyphs of Egypt?

you may work or steal your way
into the innermost shrine
and the secret escape you;

some say a bowman from the Walls
let fly the dart, some say it was Apollo,
but I, Helena, know it was Love's arrow.

But Achilles ("I tell and re-tell the story") has been an accomplice. He, as well as her own father, would have sacrificed Iphigenia. Helen returns constantly to this theme of sacrifice.

Why did he pledge her to Death?
I tell and re-tell the story
to find the answer;

it was Clytaemnestra's story,
for Iphigenia remained innocent
of the actual intent

of the lure to the altar;
as the light of the Star
glows clearer, the shadow grows darker;

his was an iron-ring
but welded to many;
Agamemnon? Menelaus? Odysseus?

were they each separately
encased in the iron-armour,
was each Typhon, a Whirlwind of War?

what did we know of any
of our Lords' activities?
we lived alone and apart.

The dream? The veil? Helen is still concerned with Achilles'
question. "I have not answered his question." She has tried to
answer the question by returning to an intermediate dimension or
plane, living in fantasy, the story of her sister. Death? Love? The
problem remains insoluble. Does it? No. The mind can not an-
swer the "numberless questions" but the heart "encompasses the
whole of the undecipherable script," when it recalls the miracle,
"Achilles' anger" and "this Star in the night."

Clytaemnestra gathered the red rose,
Helen, the white,
but they grew on one stem,

one branch, one root in the dark;
I have not answered his question,
which was the veil?

which was the dream?
was the dream, Helen upon the ramparts?
was the veil, Helen in Egypt?

I wander alone and entranced,
yet I wonder and ask
numberless questions;

the heart does not wonder?
the heart does not ask?
the heart accepts,

encompasses the whole
of the undecipherable script;
take, take as you took

Achilles' anger, as you flamed
to his Star,
this is the only answer;

there is no other sign nor picture,
no compromise with the past;
yet I conjure the Dioscuri,

those Saviours of men and of ships,
guide Achilles,
grant Clytaemnestra peace.

6

But there is a way out. A memory or race-memory prompts her.
Or even if she had been in Troy, a rumour of this story might have
reached her. Achilles would have sacrificed "his bride" to Death,
but under compulsion, and at the command of the Greek sooth-
sayer, Calchas. Is Calchas here a substitute or double of the orig-
inal Command? In any case, the iron-ring, the body-guard of
Myrmidons surrounding Achilles, accept the dictate as final.
Achilles himself, Helen argues, would have been stoned to death
by the "elect," if he had tried to rescue Iphigenia. This argu-
ment, on the material plane, justifies Achilles and Helen would
call him back.

How does the Message reach me?
do thoughts fly like the Word
of the goddess? a whisper —

(my own thought or the thought of another?)
"the Myrmidons, his own men,
would have slain him

had he attempted to thwart
the prophecy and the command
of Calchas, the priest;

the ships shall never leave Aulis,
until a virgin is offered
to Artemis; even at the last,

the Myrmidons, his elect,
would have stoned him to death;
he stood armed at the altar";

I swerve about to surprise
this Presence, this Voice,
but the long arcade is empty;

has Nephthys stepped from her pillar
or her frame upon the Wall?
is it Nemesis? is it Astarte?

who are you? where are you?
I call Achilles but not even an echo
answers, Achilles:

Achilles, Achilles come back,
you alone have the answer;
the dream? the veil?

is it all a story?
a legend of murder and lust,
the revenge of Orestes,

the death of my sister,
the ships and the Myrmidons,
the armies assembled at Aulis?

[7]

*For she suddenly feels alone. She would share her happiness,
she would proclaim the miracle, she would re-establish the Egyptian Mysteries in Greece, she would pledge herself anew to Achilles' work, "to keep and maintain the Pharos," and to the "sea-
enchantment in his eyes."*

Surely, I am not alone,
there must be priestess or priest,
there must be a family

of this ancient Dynasty,
a Pharaoh and a Pharaoh's wife?
have I imprisoned myself

in my contemplation?
has my happiness set me apart
from the rest of Egypt?

Achilles said, he had work to do,
to reclaim the coast,
to keep and maintain the Pharos,

a light and a light-house for ships,
for others like ourselves,
who are not shadows nor shades,

but entities, living a life
unfulfilled in Greece:
can we take our treasure,

the wisdom of Amen and Thoth,
back to the islands,
that enchantment may find a place

where desolation ruled,
and a warrior race,
Agamemnon and Menelaus?

But even now, it is not enough. She seems to have identified herself with her own daughter, Hermione, with her sister's daughter, Iphigenia, and with Clytaemnestra, her twin-sister, "one branch, one root in the dark." Now she seems to equate Orestes, her sister's son, with Achilles. She had said of Achilles, "let me love him, as Thetis his mother." Now of Orestes, "has he found his mother? will he ever find her? can I take her place?" She would re-create the whole of the tragic scene. Helen is the Greek drama. Again, she herself is the writing.

Hermione and Iphigenia
are protected,
they need no help;

but what of Orestes,
my sister's son, my son,
driven by Fate,

pursued by the Furies?
has he found his mother?
will he ever find her?

can I take her place?
I will wait but not forever;
I will pray by the temple lake;

Achilles will find me there,
where flower upon sacred flower,
await the coming of Light;

I will watch and wonder,
lost in an ecstasy,
awaiting the Miracle,

the Sun's beneficent weight
unclosing, disclosing each star . . .
nenuphar by nenuphar.

Book Seven

[1]

Phoenix, the symbol of resurrection has vanquished indecision and doubt, the eternal why *of the Sphinx. It is Thetis (Isis, Aphrodite) who tells us this, at last, in complete harmony with Helen.*

Choragus:
(Image or
Eidolon
of Thetis)

A woman's wiles are a net;
they would take the stars
or a grasshopper in its mesh;

they would sweep the sea
for a bubble's iridescence
or a flying-fish;

they would plunge beneath the surface,
without fear of the treacherous deep
or a monstrous octopus;

what unexpected treasure,
what talisman or magic ring
may the net find?

frailer than spider spins,
or a worm for its bier,
deep as a lion or a fox

or a panther's lair,
leaf upon leaf, hair upon hair
as a bird's nest,

Phoenix
has vanquished
that ancient enemy, Sphinx.

2

Helen with her brothers shall be deified, because of that "Love,
begot of the Ships and of War."

The Lords have passed a decree,
the Lords of the Hierarchy,
that Helen be worshipped,

be offered incense
upon the altars of Greece,
with her brothers, the Dioscuri;

from Argos, from distant Scythia,
from Delos, from Arcady,
the harp-strings will answer

the chant, the rhythm, the metre,
the syllables H-E-L-E-N-A;
Helena, reads the decree,

shall be shrined forever;
in Melos, in Thessaly,
they shall honour the name of Love,

begot of the Ships and of War;
one indestructible name,
to inspire the Scribe and refute

the doubts of the dissolute;
this is the Law,
this, the Mandate:

let no man strive against Fate,
Helena has withstood
the rancour of time and of hate.

3

Clytaemnestra? This is a different story, perhaps to be continued or consummated in another way, in another world, perhaps to be presided over by another goddess, not Nemesis nor Nephthys, "but perhaps Astarte will recall her ultimately."

Clytaemnestra struck with her mind,
with the Will-to-Power,
her Lord returned with Cassandra,

and she had a lover;
does it even the Balance
if a wife repeats a husband's folly?

never; the law is different;
if a woman fights,
she must fight by stealth,

with invisible gear;
no sword, no dagger, no ~~spear~~
in a woman's hands

can make wrong, right;
do not strive to re-weave, ~~Helen~~,
the pattern the Fates decree,

97

or tangle the threads of Nemesis;
she is not Nemesis, as you named her,
nor Nephthys, but perhaps Astarte

will re-call her ultimately;
neither she nor her son,
by a sword or a dagger's thrust,

could alter the course of a Star,
glowing by turns as ice, by turns, as fire,
Agamemnon and the Trojan War.

[4]

Clytaemnestra's problem or Clytaemnestra's "war" was not Helen's, but her Lord Agamemnon and Achilles have the iron-ring of the war or the death-cult in common. But Agamemnon, after the war and his rape or concubinage of Cassandra, the priestess of Apollo, meets dishonourable death, while Achilles falls before the Scaean Gate, with the "flash in the heaven at noon that blinds the sun," Helen upon the Walls.

The War is over and done
for us in the precinct;
the war she endured was different,

yet her Lord resembled Achilles;
when they reach a certain degree,
they are one, alike utterly;

could they have chosen
another way, another Fate?
each could — Agamemnon, Achilles,

but would they?
they would not;
but the Balance sways,

another Star appears,
as they step from the gold
into the iron-ring;

as a flash in the heaven at noon
that blinds the sun,
is their Meeting.

5

Helen had said, "I would change my place for hers, wherever she is," but the legendary King of Egypt reveals the future, the mystery or the legend. That "flash in the heaven at noon that blinds the sun" claims Helen, while Clytaemnestra is "called to another Star."

She was Mistress of Magic,
you are Mistress of Fate;
are they the same? is there another?

I listened and heard you speak,
and Achilles answer you;
I could not follow your thoughts,

but Proteus revealed to me
your past, the tale of Troy,
your legend, your history;

Proteus enchanted me,
he disclosed the mystery;
when they reach a certain degree,

they are one, alike utterly,
though Achilles woke from the dark,
and her Lord was cast

101

into the lowest depth
of Cimmerian night;
yet even Cimmerian embers,

burnt out, extinguished and lost,
will flame anew if God
wills to re-kindle the spark;

God willed that Helena
be joined to Achilles,
that Clytaemnestra

be called to another Star,
Ashtoreth, Ishtar,
Astarte . . .

6

"Helena *shall remain one name, inseparable*" *with the names of the twin-stars or the star-host,* "*the thousand-petalled lily.*"

Be still, I say, strive not,
yourself to annul the decree;
you can not return to the past

nor stay the sun in his course;
be still, I say, why weep?
you spoke of your happiness,

I was near you and heard you speak;
I heard you question Achilles
and Achilles answer you;

be still, O sister, O shadow;
your sister, your shadow was near,
lurking behind the pillars,

counting the fall of your feet,
as Achilles beneath the ramparts;
you spoke and I heard you speak;

I heard you call to your sister,
I heard you conjure her name
and the name of the Dioscuri;

be at peace, I have learned of the priests
the decree of your destiny;
I have talked with Proteus — or —

another (whoever he be,
he manifests variously);
Nameless-of-many-Names he decrees

that *Helena* shall remain
one name, inseparable
from the names of the Dioscuri,

who are not two but many,
as you read the writing, the script,
the thousand-petalled lily.

7

But only if she accepts, without reservation and without question, the decree of the Absolute, the King of Egypt, Proteus or Amen, "the Nameless-of-many-Names."

Seek not another Star,
O Helen, loved of War,
seek not to know

too much; the painted script,
the scroll, the hieroglyph
is written clear,

the sail is set,
the ship waits in the harbour;
grieve not for Clytaemnestra,

for the Fates
have woven royal purple for her bed,
have un-crowned her unhappy head;

she sleeps, call not, awake
no soul to doom
of old remembered hates;

the Nameless-of-many-Names
(Amen, you called him here)
will re-inform, habilitate, re-make

his own, even the lost, even the intemperate;
asleep? awake? a phantom or a dream,
Helen, the sails are set.

[8]

The Dream? The Veil? Obviously, Helen has walked through time into another dimension. But the timeless, hieratic symbols can be parallelled with symbols in-time. Helen herself had realized this, on her first meeting with Achilles, "the shape of this bird is a letter, they call it the hieroglyph." There are other hieroglyphs, Thetis has reminded her, a grasshopper, a flying fish, an octopus — these are Greek symbols of a Greek sea-goddess — "Helen — come home."

Strive not to wake the dead;
the incomparable host
with Helen and Achilles

are not dead, not lost;
the isles are fair (nor far),
Paphos, the Cyclades;

a simple spiral-shell may tell
a tale more ancient
than these mysteries;

dare the uncharted seas,
Achilles waits, and life;
beyond these pylons and these gates,

is magic of the wind, the gale;
the mystery of a forest-tree,
whispering its secrets upon Cithaeron,

holds subtler meaning
than this written stone
or leaves of the papyrus;

let rapture summon
and the foam-flecked sand,
and wind and hail,

rain, sleet and the bewildering snow
that lifts and falls,
conceals, reveals,

(the actual
and the apparent veil),
Helen — come home.

LEUKÉ

(*L'isle blanche*)

Book One

[1]

Why Leuké? Because here, Achilles is said to have married Helen who bore him a son, Euphorion. Helen in Egypt did not taste of Lethe, forgetfulness, on the other hand; she was in an ecstatic or semi-trance state. Though she says, "I am awake, no trance," yet she confesses, "I move as one in a dream." Now, it is as if momentarily, at any rate, the dream is over. Remembrance is taking its place. She immediately reminds us of her "first rebellion" and the so far suppressed memory and unspoken name —
Paris.

I am not nor mean to be
the Daemon they made of me;
going forward, my will was the wind,

(or the will of Aphrodite
filled the sail, as the story told
of my first rebellion;

the sail, they said,
was the veil of Aphrodite),
and I am tired of the memory of battle,

I remember a dream that was real;
let them sing Helena for a thousand years,
let them name and re-name Helen,

I can not endure the weight of eternity,
they will never understand
how, a second time, I am free;

he was banished, as his mother dreamed
that he (Paris) would cause war,
and war came.

And now she is back with the old dilemma — who caused the war? She has been blamed, Paris has been blamed but, fundamentally, it was the fault of Thetis, the mother of Achilles. There is the old argument regarding mésalliance, *a goddess marries a mortal, some social discord is sure to arise. The traditional uninvited guest introduces the fatal apple of discord. But Helen outlives, as it were, her own destiny and "Helen's epiphany in Egypt."*

Was it Paris who caused the war?
or was it Thetis? the goddess
married a mortal, Peleus;

the banquet, the wedding-feast
lacked nothing, only one uninvited guest,
Eris; so the apple was cast,

so the immortals woke to petty strife
over the challenge, *to the fairest;*
surely, the gods knew

that Thetis was fairer than Helen,
but the balance swayed
and Thetis was a goddess,

and Helen, half of earth,
out-lived the goddess Helen
and Helen's epiphany in Egypt.

111

There is more to it. She would have taken the "wisdom of Thoth" or of Egypt "back to the islands." Now on Leuké, l'isle blanche, she would reconstruct the Greek past. Thetis had said, "Achilles waits," but he must wait a little longer. He was given to her with the mystery, the miracle, in another dimension, in Egypt. But there is this world of which Thetis had spoken, of forest-trees, involuted sea-shells, snow. Helen had lived here before. In the light of her inheritance as neophyte or initiate, she would re-assess that first experience. It is true that Love "let fly the dart" that had sent Achilles to her, but it was Paris who was the agent, medium or intermediary of Love and of Troy's great patron, Apollo, the god of Song.

He would set the Towers a-flame;
Hecuba's second son would undo
the work of his father, Priam,

and of his brother, the valiant
first-born, Hector;
was this, was this not true?

they met, Hector and Achilles,
and Achilles slew Hector,
but later, a bowman from the Walls

let fly the dart;
some said it was Apollo,
but I, Helena, knew it was Love's arrow;

it was Love, it was Apollo, it was Paris;
I knew and I did not know this,
while I slept in Egypt.

*Surely, her former state was perfect, but now the temple or the
tomb, the infinite is reduced to a finite image, a "delicate sea-
shell." It is Thetis who has given this image to her, "a simple
spiral-shell may tell a tale more ancient than these mysteries."*

O the tomb, delicate sea-shell,
rock-cut but frail,
the thousand, thousand Greeks

fallen before the Walls,
were as one soul, one pearl;
I was asleep,

part of the infinite,
but there is another,
resilient as fire — Paris? Achilles?

*But Thetis? She has summoned Helen out of Egypt with
"Achilles waits." But Helen is back in time, in memory. While
"Achilles waits," she reconstructs the early story of — "Eros?
Eris?"*

What is Achilles without war?
it was Thetis, his mother,
who planned this (bridal and rest),

but even the gods' plans
are shaped by another —
Eros? Eris?

What boat, what "skiff" has brought Helen here? And how was she brought? Was it in a dream? It seems so, for she says, "I woke to familiar fragrance."

A sharp sword divides me from the past,
yet no glaive, this;
how did I cross?

coast from coast, they are separate;
I can recall the skiff,
the stars' countless host,

but I would only remember
how I woke to familiar fragrance,
late roses, bruised apples;

reality opened before me,
I had come back;
I retraced the thorny path

but the thorns of rancour and hatred
were gone — Troy? Greece?
they were one and I was one,

I was laughing with Paris;
so we cheated the past,
I had escaped — Achilles.

*Now Helen's concern is anxiety about the Sea-goddess. This is
her island. Helen has been recalled from Egypt to a Greek union,
marriage or mystery, by Thetis' "Achilles waits, and life." But
for the moment, her overwhelming experience in Egypt must be
tempered or moderated, if, "in life," she is to progress at all. It
was Paris, in the first instance, Helen says, who "had lured me
from Sparta." Now again, Paris lures her from Sparta or from
her dedication to the Spartan ideal. She is laughing with Paris,
there are roses. She is running away, as in the scene of her "first
rebellion," to "hide among the apple-trees."*

And Thetis? she of the many forms
had manifested as Choragus,
Thetis, lure-of-the-sea;

will she champion?
will she reject me?
we will hide,

a hooded cloak was thrown over me,
now it is dark upon Leuké;
the same whisper had lured me from Sparta,

we will hide among the apple-trees . . .
so it was his arrow that had given me Achilles —
it was his arrow that set me free.

117

Now Paris would remind us of his early life as shepherd and "Wolf-slayer." It was his recall to Troy, (after years of banishment and obscurity) as Prince, second only to great Hector, that had caused his death. "Death dwells in the city," he tells us. He does not seem to blame this death on Helen.

Learn of me (this is Paris) —
leave obelisks and cities,
pylons and fortresses;

my dart was named Saviour,
Ida's shepherds called me
defence and protector, Wolf-slayer;

I unsheathed my long-spear,
a staff rather, thonged with a hunting-knife;
hail Saviour, farewell,

(they knew the blight),
Death awaits you
was in the herdsman's farewell,

Death dwells in the city
whispered the hail,
warned the farewell.

Book Two

[1]

Philoctetes was also a suitor of Helen. He was a friend of Hercules who had bequeathed him his bow and poisoned arrows. An oracle had declared that Troy would not be taken without the arrows of Hercules. Philoctetes had started for Troy but had been left behind, because of a festering wound, caused by snake-bite or one of his own arrows. It was the last year of the war when he was recalled; he was restored to strength and took part in the final siege, when he shot Paris. Truly, "Death dwells in the city." The wounded Paris managed to crawl back to his old home on Mount Ida, and to Oenone, his "long-deserted companion." And Oenone? Our sympathies are with her, but who can fight Fate, Destiny or Helen? Oenone has the magic power of healing but she refuses to help her old lover.

Paris: You have not heard the story of Oenone?
           at the last, Philoctetes shot me
           with a poisoned arrow,

           bequeathed him by Hercules;
           I crawled back, they were right,
           Death dwells in the city;

but Oenone, mistress of the art,
would not heal me; Oenone?
a more potent evil had stricken

my long-deserted companion,
a venom more potent than Hercules'
had poisoned her;

she would not help me,
nor could she atone afterwards,
for my death with her death;

she could not forgive,
she could not forget,
she is not here on *Leuké*.

2

And now we see how Pallas Athene, the greatest champion of the Greeks, turns against them. The war is over but in the riot of plunder and destruction, one of the Greek heroes commits the unforgivable sin of attacking a Trojan princess who has sought sanctuary at the altar. This princess is the same Cassandra whom, later, Agamemnon took with him to Mycenae. Paris refers to Cassandra as Priestess; she was in fact dedicated to prophecies which, as we all know, were never believed. Truly, Victory is a "mocking echo."

Who will forget Helen?
forever the swirling foam
threatens the ship's keel,

for Pallas remembered
insult before her altar,
Ajax and the Maiden Cassandra;

the Sea would revenge the wrong,
the Sea would take its toll,
remorseless, with Victory

as a mocking echo, from shoal
and the straits and the ground-swell;
one Priestess counted more

than all the host and the ships,
floundering and tempest-driven;
she had given the heroes rest,

but to these she was pitiless;
"did I miss glorious death on the Walls"
(they cried) "to be swept

by the waves to ignoble death?
can no prayer save? Pallas —"
but the sea answered with shock on shock

of thundering breakers,
till the goddess cried, "enough,
now bear the remnant home";

will these forget Helen?
or will Oenone, one of the many
thousand-thousand lost?

who will forget Helen?
not Paris, feverish, with the wild eyes
of Oenone watching his death.

*But now we are in King Priam's palace before the death of
Paris, or rather we are with Paris who in his delirium sees Helen
as he saw her for the last time.*

Who will forget Helen?
as she fled down the corridor,
the wounded sentry still had breath

to hiss, "adultress";
who will forget the veil,
caught on a fallen pilaster,

the shout, then breathless silence
after the gate fell,
silence so imminent,

I heard the very stuff rip
as she tore loose and ran;
who will forget Helen?

why did she limp and turn
at the stair-head and half turn back?
was it a broken sandal?

*Remembering Helen, he begs his wife to heal him. She will do
so, on one condition, "if you forget — Helen."*

Who will forget Helen?
Oenone's eyes are wild,
flecked like a wild-cat,

"adultress and witch,
such prowl through the city streets";
then I remembered the gate,

the silence,
"heal me, Oenone";
"if you forget — Helen";

who will forget Helen?
not Paris, feverish, with the wild eyes
of Oenone, watching his death.

*Paris says to Helen, "now it is dark upon Leuké," so we imag-
ine them together — we do not know where. But we see, through
the eyes of Paris, an earlier Helen. It is a vibrant, violent Helen.
This veil to which Paris refers, as well as that other, "caught on
a fallen pilaster," seems to have no occult significance, only that in
both cases they suggest finality. It is true that the "woven veil by
the portal" that Helen clutched to break her fall, was at the beginning of the drama. The shout "from the banquet-hall, 'return the
wanton to Greece'" was answered by the defiance of Paris and the
Trojan war.*

> Now it is dark upon Leuké,
> can you see, can you feel
> the woven veil by the portal
>
> that you clutched to break your fall?
> your hand was whiter than bone;
> as you clenched your fist,
>
> the knuckles shone, ivory;
> you were eaten away by fire;
> nothing could help you,
>
> not I, Paris, tearing the folds loose,
> drawing the curtain back,
> "they can not, they will not,"

for a shout rose from the banquet-hall,
"return the wanton to Greece";
do you remember how you tore

from my arms and ran?
but a sentry stood by the door;
as you dived under his spear,

barring the way; what hand
stayed your death?
what hand smothered your cry

and dragged you back?
what arm, stronger than Hercules,
sustained you?

it was a small room,
yes, a taper was burning
in an onyx jar;

so you raged;
even Oenone's later,
was a lesser anger.

6

"The veil caught on a fallen pilaster" marks the end of the
drama, and an isolated moment in time, when Helen turns *"at the
stair-head."* Paris says, *"you saw what I did not see, till I
swerved."* In that moment before Philoctetes' arrow pierces his
shoulder, he has time to wonder why Helen hesitates. He says,
"you saw what I did not see." But he heard what she did not
hear, if his inference has any meaning. Helen had gone.

Why did you limp and turn
at the stair-head and half turn back?
you saw what I did not see,

till I swerved; they knew
that Philoctetes' arrow spelt death,
so they left me — dead;

who will forget Helen?
not the host, clanging their steel
upon steel, as they rushed

in sure pursuit of the quarry,
Helena; "how do you know?"
" — she flashed as a star,

127

then vanished into the air";
" — it's only a winding stair,
a spiral, like a snail-shell";

" — a trap — let the others go — "
" — into the heart of earth,
into the bowels of death — stand back — "

" — it's only the fumes
from the camp fires without — "
" — they have fired the turrets from below,

we are ringed with fire;
follow the others or go back?"
" — go back, go back, go back . . . "

I lived
on my slice of Wall,
while the Towers fell.

7

*That is, "the story the harpers tell" says that "she was rapt
away by Hermes, at Zeus' command." There were other stories.
But Paris had seen the enemy, had heard their arguments. He
had witnessed the confusion and panic and at the end, the blackened hollow of what had once been the famous "winding-stair, a
spiral, like a snail-shell," down which Helen had fled. Yes, Paris
says, "Zeus had rapt you away," but he adds, "the harpers never
touch their strings to name Helena and Death."*

And Helen? the story the harpers tell
reached us, even here upon Leuké;
how she was rapt away

by Hermes, at Zeus' command,
how she returned to Sparta,
how in Rhodes she was hanged

and the cord turned to a rainbow,
how she met Achilles — she met Achilles?
bereft? left? a ghost or a phantom

in Egypt? (you have told me the story);
and Helena? I crawled to the marble ledge,
but the stairs were blasted away,

the Wall was black,
the court-yard empty
save for charred armour,

the only sign of the host
that had followed you down the stairs;
yes, Zeus had rapt you away,

but the harpers
never touch their strings
to name Helena and Death.

8

She died, he says, that is all there is about it. They meet here on Leuké. There is a mystery but it happens all the time. There is nothing new about it. A tree is struck down or blighted by the frost, it flowers again . . . "now it is dark upon Leuké."

I am the first in all history
to say, she died, died, died
when the Walls fell;

what mystery is more subtle than this?
what spell is more potent?
I saw the pomegranate,

blighted by winter,
I saw the flowering pomegranate
and the cleft fruit on the summer branch;

I wait for a miracle as simple,
as inevitable as this . . .
now it is dark upon Leuké.

Book Three

[1]

So Paris in some setting, we may imagine, of former intimacy,
tells Helen, "I was king." His father was killed, "Hector was
slain by Achilles." The new king had inherited more than the
ruined Walls. He said, "I lived on my slice of Wall, while the
Towers fell." With his will to live, was his will to remember
Helen. So he seeks Oenone. That minor enchantress or "wise-
woman" would heal him. But we know the lesser power or charm
can not negate or "heal" the greater. It is only the greatest of all
that can do this.

I knew you had gone,
I do not mean, the long road to Hades,
(not so long),

I knew you had gone,
as I watched for the Wain, the Bear
to climb over my ledge of Wall,

I mean, I knew you had gone,
gone utterly, as I watched for the dawn;
when the sun came, I knew

you were never satisfied,
and strength came;
I had not satisfied you;

when she finds fulfillment,
I said, she will come back;
I was feverish, I called to Oenone,

that wise-woman would heal me;
how did I crawl or fall
through the terraced breach?

what sense lead me?
I can not remember,
only that it was empty,

a blasted shell, my city, my Wall;
I was king, Hector was slain by Achilles;
my father was slain by Pyrrhus,

Achilles' son; Achilles?
the stone was cool;
how long had I lain there?

2

So, in extremis, *the goddess appears to him. We can not be-*
lieve that Aphrodite really wants him to forget Helen. It seems
that she is testing him when she says, "I even I may recall you to
life, if you forget — Helen."

She was fair,
I had seen her before,
once upon Ida;

a tattered garment folded
across my knee,
as she bent over me;

"you are poor"; "never richer,
King of Troy, Lord of Illium;
do you regret, now all is lost,

the Judgement of Paris?"
(did Oenone see her?)
there was the lantern,

on its peg by the door,
I had taken to the sheep-fold;
"we are old, Paris, you and I,

but the mountain Ida is older;
you will come back to Ida,
your mother, you will reclaim

the kingdom, Wolf-slayer;
I even I may recall you to life,
if you forget — Helen."

3

Paris says to the apparition, "you are poor." Paris had re-turned to his shepherd's hut or cottage. "There was the lantern on its peg by the door, I had taken to the sheep-fold." It was the shepherd Paris who was chosen by Fate to award the apple. The apparition asks, "do you regret, now all is lost, the Judgement of Paris?" Paris is now the dead or dying King, the Adonis of legend. As she "walked to the door," the apparition whispered, "Leuké, the white island." *It is as if she were again offering Paris the most beautiful woman in the world — only this time, it is* l'isle blanche.

Wolf-slayer? it was my arrow
that had found Achilles' heel,
so I laughed; he had slain

Hector, my older brother
and made me King;
so I spoke to her,

and Oenone stood opposite,
dazed with wonder,
"did you call me?"

136

"no, I spoke to another
of a far land (not so far),"
for she whispered "*Leuké, the white island*,"

as she walked to the door,
yes, walked, lifting the latch softly;
she did not vanish in fire,

nor fade into the air,
she was simple,
being god-like and poor;

who will forget Helen?
not Paris, feverish, with the wild eyes
of Oenone watching his death.

4

*Again the veil motif, Paris calls it a scarf. Achilles had used
both words for the "transparent folds . . . in the beginning." The
veil? the dream? Paris would convince Helen that Achilles "was
never your lover." Paris would "break this spell," and "enter into
a circle of new enchantment."*

Was it Thetis
who lured you from Egypt?
or was it Aphrodite?

no matter, there is one law;
as the tides are drawn to the shore,
the lover draws the beloved,

as a magnet, a lode-stone, a lode-star;
a path is made on the water
for the caravel,

(they called his bark, you said, a caravel),
you drew Achilles to Egypt;
I watched you upon the ramparts,

I saw your scarf flutter
out toward the tents;
the wind? the will of Helena?

the will of Aphrodite?
no matter — there was no pulse in the air,
yet your scarf flew,

a visible sign,
to enchant him,
to draw him nearer;

whoever could break this spell,
would enter into a circle
of new enchantment;

he was father, brother,
he was deserted husband,
he was never your lover;

do not answer me, Helen;
you fell on his spear,
like a bird out of the air.

Such love, "lightning out of a clear sky," argues Paris, de-stroys not only the love-object but itself as well. And now we find, actually, that Paris and Helen are together in "this small room . . . this haven, this peace, this return, Adonis and Cytheraea."

Or he was lightning
out of a clear sky,
or hovering eagle

to fall, to tear, to devour;
you courted annihilation,
but he could not vanquish you,

nor could Helen destroy Helen;
who laid the snare?
was it Love, was it War?

what is Helen without the spears,
what is Love without arrows?
this — flickering of pine-cones,

this fragrance of pine-knots,
this small room,
no blaze of torches,

no trumpet-note, no clamour of war-gear,
this haven, this peace, this return,
Adonis and Cytheraea.

But Paris is not wholly satisfied. He feels that Helen is still under the spell of "Egyptian incense wafted through infinite corridors." He reminds her of her vow in Priam's palace, "never, never to return" and their defiance of "Achilles and the thousand spears." Again, he recalls the simple mystery of the "flowering pomegranate." Helen, he tells us (and her) in Rhodes, is Dendritis, *"Helena of the trees."*

You died in Troy on the stairs,
one does not die here;
you slipped from a husk

or a web, like a butterfly;
they call you *Dendritis* in Rhodes,
Helena of the trees;

not lightning out of the clear skies,
but waiting for the sap to rise;
why, why do you yearn to return?

I sense through the fragrance
of pine-cones, Egyptian incense
wafted through infinite corridors;

why, why would you deny
the peace, the sanctity
of this small room,

the lantern there by the door?
why must you recall
the white fire of unnumbered stars,

rather than that single taper
burning in an onyx jar,
where you swore

never, never to return,
("*return the wanton to Greece*"),
where we swore together

defiance of Achilles
and the thousand spears,
we alone would compel the Fates,

we chosen of Cytheraea;
can you forget the pact?
why would you recall another?

O Helena, tangled in thought,
be Rhodes' Helena, *Dendritis*,
why remember Achilles?

7

*He has asked, "why remember Achilles?" and apparently,
Helen has turned on him with the accusation that it is he who
has "recalled the past." There is despair and envy in him,
"hatred, fear of the Greeks." There is that shadow, that prescience, even now in "this haven, this peace, this return." He is
"defeated even upon Leuké." For her, there was "healing . . .
death or awakening . . . the love of Achilles." The final retort of
Paris is, "I say he never loved you."*

You say it is I, I who recall the host,
the flight to the stair-head,
the trampling of shod feet,

the rasp of iron-edged sandals on marble,
the shout, even before I turned, *Helena*,
the arrow you saw before I swerved,

the dart's curve; then the long descent,
the intricate spiral of the tower-stairs,
rush down? turn back?

you say it is I, I defeated even upon Leuké,
you feel in me even now, the shadow, the prescience,
envy, hatred, fear of the Greeks;

you say I have recalled the past,
and for that past, there was only one healing
(appeasement, death or awakening,

anodyne, incense) for the initiate,
(after the inevitable sequence of long tortures,
long waiting), the Mysteries of Egypt;

you say you did not die on the stairs,
that the love of Achilles sustained you;
I say he never loved you.

8

*Helen appears "in rent veil." When Aphrodite had appeared
to him in his delirium, Paris had said, "a tattered garment folded
across my knee, as she bent over me." Now Helen's garment or
"veil" is "rent." Is the garment of the apparition synonymous
with the "veil" of Helen? Is the "torn garment" in both cases, a
symbol? Paris has accepted and must accept "a tattered garment"
or an incomplete or partial manifestation of the vision, but Helen
was suave and elegant, her "garment sheathed" her, as she
"stepped from the painted prow." He says, "your sandal shone
silver, by that, I knew you who would know you anywhere." But
now, she has taken on the attributes of another. True, Paris had
referred to himself and Helen as "Adonis and Cytheraea." But
now he turns on her, "do you dare impersonate Her?" Helen is
leaving him. We feel that she has renounced, with her "silver
sandals," all claim to the world and her past affiliations with it.
She walks, "barefoot toward the door."*

Was Her power nothing that you dare
to appear there before me,
in torn garment, in rent veil?

you were suave in the dusk,
as you stepped from the painted prow
toward the rowers' tier,

your sandal shone silver;
by that, I knew you
who would know you anywhere;

you were suave but not simple,
your garment sheathed you
like an image in Egypt;

how long have we been here?
if I recalled Oenone,
I named another; are you that other

or do you dare impersonate Her?
you who were suave and cool,
with silver sandals, now walk

barefoot toward the door;
stop; vanish into thin air;
break the charm;

dissolve like fire;
do not repeat
Aphrodite's inimitable gesture.

Book Four

[1]

So Helen finds her way to another lover, whose story is not so familiar to us as that of Paris and the early suitors. For Helen, we gather, was a child when Theseus, the legendary king and hero, stole her from Sparta. He had left Helen with his mother when he went to help his friend, Pirithoüs, steal Persephone from Hades. "We had sworn each to wed only God's daughters, Swan-Helen and Eleusinian Persephone." During the absence of Theseus on this "mad adventure," the Dioscuri, Helen's brothers, rescue her and take her home again.

Theseus: How did you get here, Helen,
        do you know,
        blown by the wind, the snow?

        come here, come near;
        are you a phantom,
        will you disappear?

        will the brazier dissolve you?
        do you fear the embers?
        I am Theseus, do you remember?

        I left you with Aethra, my mother;
        what became of her?
        the Dioscuri made her your servant

when they took you back —
aië — fool that I was,
I was absent on a mad adventure,

the theft of Persephone
from Hades, in return for the help
that Pirithoüs had given me,

in stealing you from Sparta;
we had sworn, each, to wed only
God's daughters, Swan-Helen

and Eleusinian Persephone;
I escaped Pluto's rage,
but Pirithoüs was held prisoner;

then the Minotaur, Ariadne, the Labyrinth,
Hippolyta and the Amazons,
Phaedra of Crete;

these are names only,
where do they go, our old loves,
when love ceases?

and you? look — yes — you are here —
did you love me in Aphidnae,
where I left you with Aethra, my mother?

you must have loved me a little,
frail maiden that you still were,
when your brothers found you.

2

Theseus outlines this story and, philosophically, his other better known adventures. The love-stories, he tells us, have grown dim and distant, but the memory of the heroes, the Quest and the Argo is still vivid and inspiring. Helen appears "blown by the wind, the snow" and her garments cling to her, Theseus says, "like the carven folds of the Pallas, but frayed." Though driven by the wind and snow, Helen seems to have taken on something of the attributes of the Athenian goddess, and of her "olive-wood statue that directed the Quest." Perhaps she also reminds Theseus of his former encounter with Hippolyta, the devotee of Artemis, in her "huntsman's boots."

That is the law here,
perhaps everywhere, I do not know;
(come, shake the snow from your mantle,

if you fear my touch;
a shepherd's cloak?)
that is the law here, perhaps everywhere,

that only Love, the Immortal,
brings back love to old-love,
kindles a spark from the past;

I had almost forgotten you, Helen,
but, in love, I was insecure,
only the heroes remained,

the Quest and the Argo;
stand there, stand there,
are you the Palladium,

the olive-wood statue
that directed the Quest?
you are older, your garments cling to you,

(now you have dropped your mantle),
like the carven folds of the Pallas,
but frayed, and your delicate feet

wear huntsman's boots;
where have you been? what brought you here?
what kept you there in the cold?

3

But Helen must relinquish her borrowed cloak and "huntsman's gear." She is baffled and buffeted and very tired.

This is Athens, or was or will be;
do not fear, I will not immolate you
on an altar; all myth, the one reality

dwells here; take this low chair;
so seated, you are Demeter;
it was her daughter, your sister

that lost me Helena; all, all the flowers
of Enna are in your tears;
why do you weep, Helen?

what cruel path have you trod?
these heavy thongs,
let me unclasp them;

did you too seek Persephone's
drear icy way to Death?
your feet are wounded

with this huntsman's gear;
who wore these clumsy boots?
there — there — let the fire cheer you;

will you choose from the cedar-chest there,
your own fleece-lined shoes?
or shall I choose for you?

4

*"A goddess speaks," says Theseus. But it is rather the child
Helen who says, "I wanted to come home." She has quarrelled
with Paris, she has left Achilles, though she had "found perfection in the Mysteries." There is some readjustment to be made.
Symbolically, Theseus unclasps the "heavy thongs" and finds that
Helen's "feet are wounded." But Theseus will laugh at her and
her presumptions and her borrowed "gear." He will find fleece-
lined shoes for her, the glowing embers in his brazier will revive
her, together they will forget and together they will remember.*

A goddess speaks; so throned
before an altar-fire (my brazier here),
a goddess dares reveal her soul;

"in all my search" (she says),
"the shadow followed the star;
it was the same everywhere;

I wanted to come home,
I found Paris"; "Paris?"
"I can not go on, on, on

telling the story
of the Fall of Troy;
do you know Achilles?"

"was he with us on the Argo?"
"I do not know;
Love is insensate and insatiable,

I found perfection in the Mysteries,
but I was home-sick for familiar trees,
I wanted to hear the wind, to feel

snow, to embrace an ancient
twisted pine, so I walked
a long way up a mountain

he called Ida;
I found in the out-shed,
when I passed the threshold,

this cloak, he was a shepherd,
and my feet, bruised in the dark,
seemed of themselves to find

these clumsy shoes;
laugh if you are Theseus,
and I think you are,

for you laughed once,
finding a Maiden
(Helena she was)

entangled in the nets
your huntsmen spread";
" — you spoiled our quarry — "

" — but to free the birds — "
" — and found yourself entangled — "
" — that is Love."

[5]

There is the paradox of the years. Helen and Paris, in time, are about the same age. But Helen, having crossed the threshold into Egypt, finds on her return (though she says, "I shed my years on Leuké") that she is incomparably older in perception and under-standing than her former lover. The noble hero-king Theseus will find the solution for her. "All myth, the one reality dwells here."

Laugh if you are Theseus, and I think you are,
(who wore these fur-edged shoes before?)
laugh Theseus, slay another Minotaur;

do the mysteries untangle
but to re-weave?
no, I do not grieve,

I am not really crying,
I lost the Lover, Paris,
but to find the Son;

old, old, old, are the Mysteries,
though I shed my years on Leuké,
as I dropped this mantle here,

my heart had been frozen, melted,
re-moulded, re-crystallized
in the fires of Egypt,

or in the fire of Death,
the funeral-pyre of the Greek heroes;
they the many, the One

were born of myself and Achilles,
our Son; but there is another,
single, alone, proud and aloof,

no Greek but a Trojan;
he hated Achilles; Achilles
was not his father,

nor was I, Hecuba, his mother;
did he hate Hecuba?
she exposed him on Ida,

like Oedipus, to die;
tell me, god-father,
how can I be his mother?

6

How reconcile Trojan and Greek? It is Helen's old and Helen's own problem. Truly, on Leuké, the dead must be reconciled, the slayer with the slain. Achilles? Paris? Trojan and Greek arrow alike, must be re-dedicated. For as Theseus says, we are "weary of War, only the Quest remains."

It is one thing, Helen, to slay Death,
it is another thing to come back
through the intricate windings of the Labyrinth;

the heart? ember, ash or a flower,
you are Persephone's sister;
wait — wait — you must wait in the winter-dark;

you say it is not dark here?
you say the embers make happy pictures
and he reminded you of Troy;

there was a fight on the stairs?
that is all you remember,
it was all a dream until Achilles came;

and this Achilles?
in a dream, he woke you,
you were awake in a dream;

you say this waking dream
was enough, until his mother came,
Thetis or another — it was his mother

who summoned you here;
is it her island, Leuké,
or is it Aphrodite's? no matter,

belovèd Child, we are together,
weary of War,
only the Quest remains.

But Theseus, the legendary hero-king of Athens, in endeavour-
ing to help Helen answer her own questions and "reconcile Trojan
and Greek," seems inclined in spite of or perhaps because of the
Argo and the Quest, to sympathize with the Trojan rather than
with the Greek cause. He asks of Paris, "why did he hate Achil-
les?" and answers, "he hated the blight of the spears and Troy-
town taken."

Paris was Cypris' favourite, you say,
therefore, he is her son, Eros,
or if you will, Adonis, they are one;

you, Helen, could never fight Love,
why did you run away? but I am glad
his anger brought you here;

come closer, draw nearer to Theseus,
until this heart-storm is over;
Paris will find you again, never fear;

why did he hate Achilles?
you must know the answer,
he hated his rival in War,

he hated the blight of the spears
and Troy-town taken; how could it be other
if he was your first Lover?

Theseus senses the danger of Helen's recapitulation to her own apotheosis. "It is one thing, Helen to slay Death, it is another thing to come back." She has come back, she has spoken of Paris as Eros-Adonis — "what scarlet, what purple, what fire," Theseus exclaims. But Helen contradicts him, the fire is "brighter than the sun at noon-day, yet whiter than frost." Again, this is the "flash in the heaven at noon that blinds the sun." Theseus realizes that "it was all a dream until Achilles came," but he would recall, re-vitalize and re-awaken Helen. "Even a Spirit loves laughter, did you laugh with Achilles? No."

What flower from the wan water?
nenuphar, you say;
what flower with a crown of gold

or a heart or a core or a zone,
a flower within a flower;
what scarlet, what purple, what fire

of rose and bright cyclamen;
none of those, none of those, you say,
but brighter than the sun,

brighter than the sun at noon-day,
yet whiter than frost,
whiter than snow,

whiter than the white drift of sand
that lies like ground shells,
dust of shells —

— dust of skulls, I say;
what beauty, what rapture, what danger,
too great a suspense to endure,

too high the arrow, too taut the bow,
even a Spirit loves laughter,
did you laugh with Achilles? No.

Book Five

[1]

Helen must be re-born, that is, her soul must return wholly to her body. Her emotional experience has been "too great a suspense to endure." Theseus recalls names from his own past, Ariadne, Phaedra, Hippolyta, as if to balance or match Helen's Menelaus, Paris, Achilles "with bones or stones for counters." But "of the many, many in-between?" he asks. "The memory of breath-taking encounters with those half-seen" must balance and compensate for the too intense primary experience.

There was always another and another and another,
shall we match them like knuckle-players
with bones or stones for counters,

the fatality of numbers?
the first? the last?
and of the many, many in-between,

importunate, breath-taking encounters
with those half-seen,
the wind billowing a sail

and the sail fluttering
and one half-balanced,
drawing the sail taut,

and then the sail is lost,
and we have only guessed
or half-guessed

at the turn of a head,
whose was the ensign (painted on the prow)
of one whose name, even, will be

an eternal enigma;
who was it? who did I see?
was this the embodiment of the host,

the lost, Ariadne, Phaedra, Hippolyta?
or was it Helen on the way to Egypt,
or was it Helen returning,

or was it Helen on the sea-road,
nearing Troy? was it one of these
or all three? reflections . . .

and a head half-turned to watch
a reeling tern, a sleeve,
a garment's fold, no word, no whisper,

nor glance even . . . or was it a gull
she watched, a heron or raven
or plover? the eclipsed pillar

with the shadow showing darker,
for the white gleam above,
of sun-lit marble,

a certain sheen of cloth,
a certain ankle,
a strap over a shoulder?

remember these small reliques,
as on a beach, you search
for a pearl, a bead,

a comb, a cup, a bowl
half-filled with sand,
after a wreck.

2

*Helen must remember other loves, small things, "a pearl, a
bead, a comb, a cup, a bowl," and he tells her that she must "return to the Shell, your mother, Leda, Thetis or Cytheraea." Theseus says that she is like a butterfly, "a Psyche with half-dried
wings."*

What bird, ever, was less beautiful than man?
live with the Swan, your begetter,
return to the Shell, your mother,

Leda, Thetis or Cytheraea;
Achilles or Paris?
beyond Trojan and Greek,

is the cloud, the wind, the Lover
you sought in the snow;
I am half-way to that Lover,

so rest — rest — rest —
here, we are half-way to the mountain,
the mountain beyond the mountain,

the mountain beyond Ida;
you found your way through despair,
but do not look back,

neither across the dividing seas,
to the sand and the hieroglyphs,
nor further (though nearer)

to the Towers and the blackened Walls,
there is nothing to fear,
you are neither there nor here,

but wavering
like a Psyche
with half-dried wings.

3

So as if to reassure, to strengthen this Psyche, this revenant,
*Theseus tells her his own story, and to allay her fears of "the
Towers and the blackened Walls," recalls his own primeval terror. But the Minotaur, in retrospect, was "an idle fancy, a dream,
a Centaur."*

There was always another and another and another,
these were the knots in the thread,
or rather the strands of hemp-like wool

that I stuffed into my wallet:
one knot after another,
I named them, Aethra, my mother —

who were the others?
I remembered them then,
I forgot them soon after;

those were the knots in the woof
of different texture and colour
that Daedalus gave Ariadne;

she would wait for me
at the threshold, if I ever came back
from the Monster — the Minotaur?

my child, an idle fancy,
a dream, a Centaur,
hallucination of infancy;

so we were drawn back,
back to the past,
and beyond, to the blessèd isles,

and beyond them to Lethe,
and beyond forgetfulness
to new remembrance,

and beyond the new remembrance
to the opiate of non-remembrance,
when the spark of thought goes out,

only the bliss of the immortal fields,
(they called it Death);
they had gone on, the rest,

the seven and the seven
demanded as tribute;
Crete? magic: Athens? thought,

the delight of the intellect,
but what is thought
to forgetting?

The mountain, the reality, Theseus seems to argue, must recall
us from the dream, "the opiate of non-remembrance." The magic
of Crete was inherited from Egypt. Parnassus, or Greek creative
thought, must not be entangled in the Labyrinth or dissolved or
washed away by "the ancient Nile."

Perhaps I saw him sleeping in the grass,
as gentle as Europa's noble beast;
was he myth or fiction,

an invention of Daedalus,
even as the Labyrinth?
or was it true

that I dealt him his death-blow?
and was it true, as I argued afterwards,
that I slew Egypt?

Crete would seduce Greece,
Crete inherited the Labyrinth from Egypt,
the ancient Nile would undermine

the fabric of Parnassus;
was this true? I think I named them,
knotting the bright threads,

Hymettus, Parnes, Lycabettus,
even as your Guardian (you told me)
recalled you with Cithaeron.

169

And all this time, Helen has apparently been seated before the glowing coals. "Take this low chair," Theseus had said, and now, "shall I draw out the low couch, nearer the brazier?" He will cover her with fleece or if that is too heavy, with "soft woven wool," so that she ("my Psyche") may "disappear into the web, the shell, re-integrate." She is safe, she need not be afraid "to recall the shock of the iron-Ram, the break in the Wall," or equally, she is free to forget everything. But Helen's only answer to that is "never . . . Achilles."

Rest here; shall I draw out
the low couch, nearer the brazier,
or will you lie there,

against the folds of purple
by the wall? you tremble,
can you stand? walk then,

O, sleep-walker; is this fleece
too heavy? here is soft woven wool;
wrapped in this shawl, my butterfly,

my Psyche, disappear into the web,
the shell, re-integrate,
nor fear to recall

the shock of the iron-Ram,
the break in the Wall,
the flaming Towers,

shouting and desecration
of the altars; you are safe here;
remember if you wish to remember,

or forget . . . "never, never,"
you breathe, half in a trance . . .
"Achilles."

6

*There are new names, Chryseis, Deidamia, Briseis; they seem
unrelated to our Achilles concept. Nor does the story of Polyxena,
the Trojan princess, sacrificed to placate the ghost of Achilles,
seem altogether relevant. Theseus begins "to remember the story."
It is another story. He seems deliberately to have stepped out of the
stream of our and of Helen's consciousness. Why? He has told
her that she was safe with him. He reminds her that she "found
life here with Paris." His Achilles lingering with Polyxena
("leave him with the asphodels") is not Helen's Achilles "on the
desolate beach."*

I begin to remember the story,
do I remember what you remember?
but could you know of the sacrifice

of Polyxena, Hecuba's daughter,
the sister of Paris? could you know
that Achilles desired her,

and the ghost of Achilles
demanded her sacrifice?
his son slew her;

there was Chryseis, Apollo's priestess,
and his own wife, Deidamia,
the mother of Pyrrhus,

and Briseis — and what other?
they were all sacrificed in one way or another;
after death, if his spirit desired

Polyxena, why should you imagine
that he left her? was he not content?
leave him with the asphodels,

you found life here with Paris;
you loved brother and sister,
and more (the story unfolds itself),

Pyrrhus, his son, married your daughter;
"Hermione? never, it was Orestes loved her,
the son of Clytaemnestra, my sister";

how do you know that?
can you read the past
like a scroll?

7

Helen has heard what he said but she lies "quietly as the snow, drifted outside." Theseus' words with the names of the four wo-men "sacrificed in one way or another" seem hardly to have reached her. She can only ask, "does the ember glow in the heart of the snow?" and then answer, "there is a voice within me, listen — let it speak for me."

It comes to me, lying here,
it comes to me, Helena;
do you see the cloth move,

or the folds, to my breathing?
no, I breathe quietly,
I lie quietly as the snow,

drifted outside; how did I find
the threshold? marble and snow
were one; is this a snow-palace?

does the ember glow
in the heart of the snow?
yes — I drifted here,

blown (you asked) by what winter-sorrow?
but it is not sorrow;
draw near, draw nearer;

do you hear me? do I whisper?
there is a voice within me,
listen — let it speak for me.

8

*It is an heroic voice, the voice of Helen of Sparta. The loves of
Achilles, the loves of Helen of Troy seem ephemeral and unimpor-
tant beside their passionate devotion and dedication to "the rage of
the sea, the thunder of battle, shouting and the Walls."*

Theseus, god-father, what of that other
and that other, you speak of,
the loves of Achilles?

do I care? I am past caring
and he was past caring
when he found me;

O, the surge of the sea,
O, the billows,
O, the mighty urge

of the oak-prow,
the creak of oak-beams,
the sway of the mast,

it was only a small ship, the last,
(yes, we called it a caravel),
yet it was a Ship to hold all;

did the Spirits travel with him?
or did they come before?
but listen — it is no matter,

they, Achilles and I
were past caring;
O, the rage of the sea,

the thunder of battle,
shouting and the Walls
and the arrows; O, the beauty of arrows,

each bringing surcease, release;
do I love War?
is this Helena?

Book Six

1

Again, the "voice" seems to speak for Helen. It is a lyric voice this time, a song rather than a challenge. It takes us back to Egypt but in a Greek mode. Isis is Cypris (Cytheraea) and Isis is Thetis. Amen-Zeus is the father of Isis-Thetis-Aphrodite (Cypris). We can not altogether understand this evocation, the rhythms must speak for themselves and the alliterations, Cypris, Thetis, Nephthys, Isis, Paris. Proteus, the legendary King of Egypt, as we have learned before, takes many shapes. Could he "manifest as Achilles?" If so, (the question is not asked but implied), could he manifest as Paris? Then, could the two opposites (the slayer and the slain) merge into one, and that One, the Absolute? This last question is implicit but not formulated by the final phrase or strophe, "Amen begot Amor."

Cypris, Cypria, Amor,
say the words over and over,
what does she want, this Cypris,

for Cypris is Thetis;
seek not another Star (she said),
O Helen, loved of War:

War, Ares, Achilles, Amor;
Karnak was her temple;
Amen-Zeus is her father, my father,

his temple is our temple,
there, I sought Clytaemnestra;
I called my sister, Astarte

or Nephthys, twin-sister of Isis,
and Isis is Cypris, Cypria;
what does she want? why Paris?

why does he come to haunt
my dream here, my half-trance,
my trance, Nepenthe, forgetfulness?

(say the words over and over,
Cypris, Cypria, Amor);
Paris was no friend of Achilles,

could Achilles be father of Amor,
begotten of Love and of War?
(say the words over and over);

was Proteus his father?
could Proteus, king of Egypt,
of many names, of many shapes,

manifest as Achilles?
stop — O voice prompting my strophies,
stop — how could that be?

if Thetis was Cypris, Cypria,
(you say) who could not Achilles be?
in the temple, in the dark,

in the fragrance of the incense,
without touch, without word,
by a thought, Amen begot Amor.

2

Now Helen asks the question, "must youth and maturity quar-rel?" The heroic Spartan Helen had, like the hero-king Theseus, "passed the frontier, the very threshold." Theseus had been suc-cessful in his Quest of the symbolic Golden Fleece, Helen in her Quest of Love. But in both cases, there was an enemy to be con-quered, "they called it Death." " — and then? the way out, the way back, the way home."

Paris was my youth — don't you see?
must youth and maturity quarrel
but how reconcile

the magnetic, steel-clad Achilles
with the flowering pomegranate?
in Rhodes (Paris said) they called me

Dendritis, Helena of the trees;
can spring forget winter?
there was no winter in Egypt,

but I passed the frontier,
the very threshold you crossed
when you sought out the Minotaur;

was Achilles my Minotaur?
a dream? a dream within a dream?
a dream beyond Lethe?

Crete? magic, you say,
and Crete inherited the Labyrinth,
and Crete-Egypt must be slain,

conquered or overthrown — and then?
the way out, the way back,
the way home.

[3]

So "Eros? Eris?" are again balanced in the mind of Helen, or Eros and Death.

Is there another stronger than Love's mother?
is there one other, Discordia, Strife?
Eris is sister of Ares,

his unconquerable child is Eros;
did Ares bequeath his arrows
alike to Eros, to Eris?

O flame-tipped, O searing, O tearing
burning, destructible fury
of the challenge *to the fairest;*

O flame-tipped, O searing,
destroying arrow of Eros;
O bliss of the end,

Lethe, Death and forgetfulness,
O bliss of the final
unquestioned nuptial kiss.

And Eris is this fire-brand, Paris, and Eros is again, the "un-conquerable child." How reconcile the opposites? Helen endeavours to do this, with partial success. Perhaps, for her, the transition is possible, or the "subtle genealogy." For us, "this is no easy thing to explain." The slayer becomes the son of the slain, "he is incarnate Helen-Achilles." This is perhaps a pre-vision on Helen's part of the traditional Euphorion to come. But we feel that Helen will return to her original concept or a new revelation of the "heroes slain."

Paris was cursed like Helen;
his mother dreamed of a fire-brand
and the Towers a-flame

and War came; Hecuba like Jocasta
was overthrown (by Paris, by Oedipus,
the son); O the web is sure

and Fate shall net her own,
and Fate will play another trick
like Hermes, the jester;

he of the House of the Enemy,
Troy's last king (this is no easy thing
to explain, this subtle genealogy)

is Achilles' son, he is incarnate
Helen-Achilles; he, my first lover,
was created by my last;

can you understand this?
it was not Pyrrhus, at the end,
it was not some waif of Achilles' Chryseis

or Briseis begetting, nor a ghost-child
or Polyxena; no, it was not the legitimate
Pyrrhus who slew Priam, the father of Paris,

but Paris himself, Paris whose swift arrow
(O Wolf-slayer) pierced the Achilles-heel;
alike but different, apart from the heroes slain,

but one, one other, *the* other,
incarnate, manifest Egypt;
he, the fire-brand, was born of the Star,

was engendered under the cloak
of the new-mortal Achilles;
O Thetis, O sea-mother, I prayed under his cloak,

let me remember, let me remember,
forever, this Star in the night;
it was Thetis, the sea-mother

recalled me from Egypt, with "Achilles waits";
how could I know, the fire-brand, the ember,
the Star would return — but other;

185

this is no easy thing
to understand, O god-father;
draw close, draw closer,

take my hands in your hands,
teach me to remember,
teach me not to remember.

[5]

*Helen has gone too far or not far enough. Theseus recalls her
from her abstraction, her Absolute, the "Star in the night." The
child (like Proteus-Amen) takes many forms. And in her case especially, there are the twin-brothers and the twin-sister to consider.
She is (or was) a composite of all these, "growing within the
Egg." Zeus-Amen decreed that two of the four should be born of
light, the other two of darkness. The child of light will strive to
redeem the child of darkness, "Castor received immortality through
Pollux, you sought (do you still seek?) Clytaemnestra in Egypt?"*

Helen — Helen — Helen —
there was always another and another and another;
the rose has many petals,

or if you will, the nenuphar,
father, brother, son, lover,
sister, husband and child;

beyond all other, the Child,
the child in the father,
the child in the mother,

the child-mother, yourself;
O Helena, pause and remember,
lest you return to that other

and flame out, incandescent;
remember your earthly father,
Tyndareus; some say he embraced

187

your mother, Leda, before or after
Zeus (or Amen, you called him)
laid the Swan-seed, Helena;

some say (did you know this?)
that the Swan fathered Helen and Pollux,
but that Castor and Clytaemnestra

were mortals, begot of Tyndareus;
so growing within the Egg,
you were destined forever to know

this dual companionship,
man and hero, Castor,
god and hero, Pollux,

yourself in another,
the magic of Clytaemnestra;
O tiny world, O world of infinity,

two mortals strike across
to intercept the path
of two daemons; two spirits

seek to save
the lost sister or brother;
Castor received immortality

through Pollux, you sought
(do you still seek?)
Clytaemnestra in Egypt.

Helen does not answer this last question, nor directly repudiate Theseus when he suggests that she temper her emotional intensity, lest she "flame out, incandescent." Rather, she compares Theseus with Achilles, and asks, "how have the arcs crossed? how have the paths met?"

Achilles, the man-hero,
Theseus, the god-hero,
that is clear enough;

my brother, Castor,
my brother, Pollux,
twin-star to guide ships;

Achilles with the mermaid,
Thetis at the prow,
be-calmed at Aulis;

Theseus with the Argo,
valiant in the Quest;
Achilles vanquished before Troy,

Theseus, ever-victorious;
how have the arcs crossed?
how have the paths met?

How indeed? Theseus answers her. It seems that Theseus and Achilles, like Castor and Pollux, are twin-stars, or "a twin-star to guide ships." They meet as opposites meet, dark-light, life-death, death-life and so on. They meet finally in "Helen in Egypt" and "Helen in Hellas forever."

Thus, thus, thus,
as day, night,
as wrong, right,

as dark, light,
as water, fire,
as earth, air,

as storm, calm,
as fruit, flower,
as life, death,

as death, life;
the rose deflowered,
the rose re-born;

Helen in Egypt,
Helen at home,
Helen in Hellas forever.

And Helen understands, though we do not know exactly what it is that she understands. To her, "it is all very simple." She says, "it was darkness, Achilles and war, it was light with the Argo, the Quest."

Isis, yes Cypris, the cypress,
the Tomb of Amor,
the Tomb of Love;

yes — it breaks, the fire,
it shatters the white marble;
I see it, suddenly I see it all,

the Shell, the Tomb, the Crystal,
Tyndareus, my earth-father, and Zeus
or Zeus-Amen in heaven,

and I am only a daughter;
no, no, I am not a mother,
let Cypris have Amor,

let Isis have Horus,
let Leda have Zeus,
and Hecuba, Priam,

and Hecuba, Paris,
and Jocasta, Oedipus,
and Jocasta, Antigone;

the Sphinx? it is clear enough;
the snow-crystal reflects
the seven arcs,

(how have the arcs met?)
it was darkness,
Achilles and war,

it was light
with the Argo, the Quest;
reconcile? reconcile?

day, night, wrong, right?
no need to untangle the riddle,
it is very simple.

Book Seven

[1]

So Helen is at peace, she has found the answer, she will rest.
Now Thetis who (like Proteus) "can change her shape," is Arte-
mis, the Moon-goddess, "her sphere is remote, white, near, is
Leuké . . . let me stay here."

Thetis is the Moon-goddess
and can change her shape,
she is Selene, is Artemis;

she is the Moon, her sphere
is remote, white, near,
is *Leuké*, is marble and snow,

is here; this is Leuké,
a-drift, a shell but held
to its central pole

or its orbit;
this is the white island,
this is the hollow shell,

this is the ship a-drift,
this is the ship at rest,
let me stay here;

is it Death to know
this immaculate purity,
security?

So there must be no rivalry with either the earth or the heaven mother. Helen says, "I am only a daughter." She will not compete with Demeter for union with her Absolute or with Leda for this same Zeus. There is another Absolute, that of "the crystal, the center, the ice-star." It is the Absolute of negation, if you will, or of completion, "this immaculate purity," and hence in a sense, of Death. Helen had said, "my heart had been frozen, melted."— So she compares herself to Persephone and recalls Theseus' question, "did you too seek Persephone's drear icy way to Death?" Helen's answer is yes, "I found or was found by Dis."

I am only a daughter,
no, I am not Demeter,
seated before an altar,

your braizer, there,
I am Koré, Persephone; you said,
did you too seek Persephone's

drear icy way to Death?
I found or was found by Dis;
no rivalry with Demeter for Zeus,

or with Leda; I was taken
but never forsaken by another,
his brother, by Hades;

O, the surge of the sea,
O, power of battle,
the wrack and the curse;

I was taken, not by Menelaus
in Sparta, not by Paris
in Troy or after,

but by Achilles;
can spring defeat winter? never;
spring may come after,

but the crystal, the center, the ice-star
dissembles, reflects the past
but waits faithful;

no, god-father,
Paris will never find me;
I reflect, I re-act, I re-live;

true, he renewed my youth,
but now, only the memory of the molten ember
of the Dark Absolute claims me

who have met Death,
who have found Dis,
who embraced Hades;

South turns North,
Hyperborean dwellings wait;
Achilles waits, she said;

he treads among the stations,
he takes his way by might,
by stealth, by cunning, by betrayal,

from star-house to house;
Achilles waits or Hercules or Osiris,
does it matter?

and do I care? only let Thetis,
the goddess hold me for a while
in this her island, her egg-shell.

3

*Achilles is "a sword-blade drawn from fire . . ." Menelaus,
Paris had not yet been "tempered." Helen seems to ask, how can I
compromise? My soul or my spirit was snatched from its body, or
even more miraculously, with its body, by this "gerfalcon." All
she asks now is "time to remember."*

Helen — Hades —
do you know his face?
it is not dark but clear,

a sword-blade drawn from fire,
tempered, beaten till it grows cold,
cold, cold, colder

than the pole-star;
do you know his eyes?
they are not dark caves,

as the priests tell,
they are sea-gray, they are the sea,
crept from under an ice-floe,

they are not frozen, no,
but they keep the gray sheen of the sea;
do you know his hands?

(was he with you on the Argo?)
they are powerful but thin;
too fine for strength?

have you seen a gerfalcon
fall on his prey?
so my throat knew that day,

his fingers' remorseless steel,
when I had strength only to pray
Thetis, *let me go out, let me forget,*

let me be lost . . .
could another touch you
after the Absolute?

hate? no; love? no;
nothingness? no, not nothingness
but an ever widening flight . . .

but I would not go yet,
I must have time to remember
Dis, Hades, Achilles.

4

She will encompass infinity by intense concentration on the mo-
ment. She has finished her cycle in time. But out-of-time or beyond
moon-time, are the "widening star-circles." But she will not at-
tempt to escape "the moment" by a flight to infinity with "wild
wings." She will bring the moment and infinity together "in time,
in the crystal, in my thought here."

Time with its moon-shape here,
time with its widening star-circles,
time small as a pebble,

with bones or stones for counters,
(what did you say?)
there was always another and another and another;

if I am small enough,
held in this smallest sphere,
this moon-crystal, this shell,

if I dare renounce spring-love,
Adonis and Cytheraea, and a small room,
a taper burning in an onyx jar,

(Paris said, *why must you recall*
the white fire of unnumbered stars,
rather than that single taper

burning in an onyx jar),
it is for another (you are right,
god-father) and another;

but the Vision is not Protean,
it is actual, unwavering,
each station separate, each line drawn,

each pillar erect,
each porch level with the rocks,
and rock-steps leading to a throne

or down to a pool, a mirror
and a reflection . . .
that is the star-way,

I will not be flung out
with wild wings,
I will bring the Hyperboreans to me,

I will encompass the infinite
in time, in the crystal,
in my thought here.

5

Time-in-time (*personal time*) however, as well as star-time
(*the eternal*) seem alike incalculable to Helen, without Achilles.
But by a miracle of re-adjustment, through her contact with Theseus, "*the Wheel is still.*" Helen says, "*the Wheel is as small as
the gold shoulder-clasp, I wore as a girl.*" Yet the Wheel is the
great circle of the Zodiac with its "*outline of hero and beast,*"
which Achilles found were still "*the familiar stars,*" as the mast
of the caravel, the death-ship measured them out, "*picture by picture.*"

> *Achilles waits*, aye,
> stepping from sphere to sphere,
> aye, the long way;
>
> he will finish his task,
> Hercules' twelve labours,
> in twelve aeons, in twelve years,
>
> in twelve days,
> aye, Hades-Hercules,
> the long way;
>
> to me, the Wheel is still,
> (hold me here),
> the Wheel is as small

as the gold shoulder-clasp,
I wore as a girl;
the Wheel is a jewel,

set in silver; to me
the Wheel is a seal . . .
the Wheel is still.

6

*So "picture by picture," Helen would read the star-script, as
Achilles had done. Paris will come back, he "will reflect the past"
and Helen as she was "before the ultimate Mystery." But Helen
in her mind, or "in my crystal" as she calls it, "would see further." She would relate the pictures in time to the pictures in
eternity, as she "strove in the precinct, to decipher the Amen-
script."*

But yes, you are right,
Paris will come back
but as the rose-light,

one segment, separate
from the prismatic seven
of the white crystal;

yes, he will come back,
the crystal will reflect the past
and that present-in-the-past,

our meeting on *Leuké;*
she is not lost,
Rhodes' Helena, *Dendritis;*

Paris found Helen
as she was before
the ultimate Mystery,

the blazing focus
of the sun-blade, the ember,
Achilles in Egypt;

but I would see further,
I would renew the Quest,
I would bind myself with the Girdle,

the circlet, the starry Zone;
as I strove in the precinct,
to decipher the Amen-script,

so I would read here
in my crystal, the Writing,
I would measure the star-space,

even as Achilles
measured the stars
with the sway of a ship's mast,

even as Achilles counted,
picture by picture,
the outline of hero and beast.

She would see and be. Though herself free from time-restrictions and the Wheel, she would endure or share the "labours" of Achilles, whatever they might be. At the same time, she "would wander through the temples of the stars." This is possible only through reflection and meditation. "What was Helena's task?" She can not altogether say, only that through the power and tenderness of Theseus, "it was finished."

I would wander through the temples
of the stars, his familiars;
I would seek, I would find,

I would endure with him,
the twelve labours,
conquer Boar, Stag, Lion;

what was Helena's task?
do we know?
only that it was finished

when she stumbled out of the snow,
across the threshold,
and found you here.

And now there is one prayer, a prayer addressed to the king-hero Theseus ("O god-father"), rather than as in the beginning, to that more distant abstraction, "Amen, All-father." The prayer will be answered, Helen knows. It is a simple prayer for Achilles, "may he find the way."

There is one prayer,
may he find the way;
O god-father, draw nearer,

help me to speed the ship,
he must sail far, far;
help me, you Master of Argo,

to re-assemble the host,
so that none of the heroes be lost,
teach me to remember,

(there is one prayer,
may he find the way),
teach me not to remember.

EIDOLON

Book One

[1]

Why eidolon? At the end of the first book, Thetis appears, or the image or eidolon of Thetis calls Helen out of Egypt. Now after the reconciliation with time, Greek time, (through the council and guidance of Theseus), Helen is called back to Egypt. It is Achilles who calls her — or it is the image or eidolon of Achilles who is "commanded to say, Theseus commands me."

Achilles: Commanded to seek other
Boar, Stag, Lion,
another Sea-monster,

another Bull, other Oxen,
other Apples, another Amazon
with her star-zone,

commanded by Formalhaut,
the Initiator, royal, sacred
High Priest of love-rites,

208

more ancient than Troy citadel;
commanded to seek you here,
for you never left Egypt;

commanded to say, in Egypt,
we are in Eleusis,
Helen is Persephone,

Achilles is Dis,
(the Greek Isis-Osiris);
commanded to pray,

as before the high-altar,
your couch here;
commanded to display

a brand, flame, torch;
commanded to say,
Theseus commands me.

2

*Achilles reminds Helen of how Thetis, in the first instance, had
summoned her with "Achilles waits." He waits, not as Lord of
Legions, "King of Myrmidons," but as one dedicated to a new
Command, that of the "royal sacred High Priest of love-rites."*

You ask how you came here;
Theseus' servants bore your couch,
silently, set down the lion-claws

on the steps; softly
as those lion-paws on sand,
Theseus and Achilles

lifted the catafalque, the bier
and you sleeping, exhausted
with the fight, your struggle

to understand *Leuké*, the light;
silently, Thetis commanded,
Thetis in her guise of mother,

who first summoned you here
with *Achilles waits;*
I waited before the frozen portal,

the gates; yes, you had come home,
but the long way (Theseus told me
of your prayer, your Wheel),

the long way (Theseus told me
of your Achilles-Hercules),
the long way was revoked

by your longing, your prayer,
I would endure with him;
Thetis summoned you here,

Theseus protected, renewed you,
not for your starry circle
in a crystal sphere,

but for the brand, burning here,
the Wheel is a seal;
Theseus revealed all your secrets.

Who is Formalhaut? We gather that this is a synonym for "the Nameless-of-many-Names," Proteus, King of Egypt. It is the same Amen-temple, at all times, in all places, on all planes of existence, whether they are symbolized by Athens, the intellect, or by Eleusis, the mysteries.

This is Formalhaut's temple,
not far from Athens,
not far from Eleusis,

yet Egypt; not far
from Theseus, your god-father,
not far from Amen, your father

but dedicated to Isis,
or if you will, Thetis;
not far from the blessèd isles,

the Hesperides, or from Amenti;
not far from life-in-death,
another portal, another symbol.

But the innermost mystery of "*life-in-death*," it seems, must be balanced or tempered by outer circumstance. Paris, or the voice or image of Paris, would call Helen back to "*my small room.*" Even before she left him to find Theseus, Paris had been apprehensive, perhaps not so much fearing the loss of Helen to Achilles, but of her final translation to the transcendent plane, the fragrance of "*Egyptian incense wafted through infinite corridors.*" Now he would denigrate the "*young hero,*" reminding Helen of the incident of Scyros. He says, "*call on Thetis.*" Is this ironical? It has been Thetis from the first, who reconciled Helen to Achilles. But Paris would reduce the valour of the hero to "*woman's robe and ornament.*"

Paris: Your moon, your shell, your crystal
was a tomb; Paris? Achilles?
you asked this,

while we rested days, nights,
in my small room;
Helen, enchantress,

are you doomed to enchantment?
a sharp sword divides me from the past,
I had escaped — Achilles;

would you go back,
would you go back
to myrrh, olibanum,

storax, sandarac,
the incense of magic?
(or what you will,

he would take you
with white-poppy,
with black-poppy,

clove, sandal;)
call on Thetis,
the sea-mother,

remember how she decked the young hero
in woman's robe and ornament,
and hid him in Scyros,

that Achilles escape Troy,
that Achilles escape death,
the arrow of Paris.

*There is challenge and defiance in Paris, as he recalls Helen's
own words to her. By tribal law, the young priest slays the old
one, the son, the father. Helen had recalled the Oedipus story in
her talk with Theseus. "It is very simple," she had said. It does
not seem simple, nor does the explanation of Paris help much. He
evidently represents a secondary order, "completing the circle, the
triangle, the broken arc." In that sense, he is the third of the inevitable triad.*

Theseus spoke; *all myth,*
the one reality dwells here;
so you are right

with Helen-Persephone,
with Pluto-Achilles;
but there was another,

incompatible in life,
yet in myth, completing the circle,
the triangle, the broken arc,

Dionysus-Paris; you were right,
he of the house of the enemy,
Troy's last king,

is Achilles' son, he is incarnate
Helen-Achilles; he my first lover
was created by my last.

Now Paris himself refers to the legend. He will accept the accredited Hero, as father-symbol, if Helen will take the place of his mother, Hecuba, the Trojan Queen, who had left him "like Oedipus to die." But first, he would rescue Helen from what he seems to consider "a death-cult." It almost seems better, he seems to say, to have a new war, "new Myrmidons," than to "call by stealth, ghosts, phantoms of old legions." Though the conventional image of Paris is of an effete youth, we must remember his claim to the title, "Wolf-slayer," and the fact that he was chosen as deputy to the god Apollo (or even as legend states, that Apollo had manifested in his image) to strike down "the greatest hero in Greece."

Pluto-Achilles — his is a death-cult
to drag you further and further underground,
underneath vault and tomb;

to rise in long corridors,
to re-read your old script?
Boar? Lion? he would sacrifice

Boar, Lion, Stag, Man,
aye, and another Hippolyta
for her star-zone;

leave him to the sea-ways,
let him re-assemble new Myrmidons,
rather than call by stealth,

ghosts, phantoms of old legions;
he would turn you to Pythoness,
Priestess — is there no magic

left above earth?
remember my arrow
that found his heel;

the brand he would proffer
is burnt-out, extinguished;
Achilles is old, his war is over;

my war? defence of the shepherd
against wolf, panther,
ravaging eagle; his war

was death of brother by brother,
blight, ruin, plague, famine;
his war? my war? . . . Helen's?

if Achilles is my father
in this new spirit-order,
I will acept the Hero

if you are my mother,
for I, I was left by Hecuba,
like Oedipus to die;

Jocasta, Oedipus? Hecuba, Paris?
this is the old story,
no new Euphorion.

7

*And now Paris repeats the names of those women whom The-
seus had told us were "sacrificed in one way or another." It is
however especially with the sacrifice of his sister, Polyxena, that
Paris is concerned. He seems to intimate that this special sacrifice might have a parallel. Polyxena was slain to propitiate a
ghost. Even the pretended marriage of Iphigenia to Achilles was
by way of a pledge "to War and the armies of Greece." Her sacrifice was to have been to a living, even if to an inimical concept.
But Polyxena's sacrifice was to one already dead, and so by im-
plication, Paris seems to say that Helen's might be.*

It was not only Iphigenia,
(you told me the story),
there was always another and another and another,

(I read all your thoughts, the words
of you and Theseus together);
remember Polyxena, golden by the altar,

remember Pyrrhus, his son slew her;
where did she wander?
O golden sister,

are you still subjugated? enchanted?
are all the slain
bound to this Master?

Achilles spoke, *Theseus commands me,*
but where is he?
do he and I stand over

a new victim? do we meet
to defraud the future
of life, light?

(yes, it was light upon *Leuké*);
remember my golden sister,
you saw her, you loved her

as your own daughter,
and I, I was that other,
Orestes, *my sister's son,*

my son, driven by Fate;
remember Clytaemnestra's
last words to Orestes,

remember Iphigenia;
remember Iphigenia,
remember Polyxena,

remember that other and that other and that other,
Briseis, Chryseis,
priestess of Apollo.

8

*Helen seems to start awake — was this dream? delirium? She
has been lying where Theseus left her, "everything is as it was
before." But she is alone, though she knows that "Theseus will
come if I call." Is the room dark? She wakes to confusion of
images, "a catafalque, a bier, a temple again." Was all her
effort for nothing? Someone has mocked her, "the script was a
snare." Where is she? In "a tomb; a small room?" Her heart, her
head are alike anguished. But now she remembers, "how I
stumbled here out of the snow." Yes, she has "come home."*

Helen: I do not see Achilles,
        Paris is far, far —
        it was a dream, a catafalque, a bier,

        a temple again, infinite corridors,
        a voice to lure, a voice to proclaim,
        the script was a snare;

        a name of incense,
        I can not remember,
        sandarac? sandal?

        my heart beating,
        my head enclosed in a ring, a band,
        someone defined as crystal

and a tomb; a small room?
a taper, a candle, then
a blaze of splendour, a brand

to flame through long halls,
we would find bliss again;
but he reviled us — who? who?

I ask myself who said this,
who spoke (if any), who answered;
was it Paris defied the kiss

of his very begetting?
a name that was foretold
would bring ruin — ruin?

it is I, Helen, who took the blame;
what flame over Troy?
no, it is only the dim glow

of the brazier; I remember,
I stumbled here out of the snow;
I sat there, I lay here,

and everything is as it was before;
Theseus will come if I call;
what flame over Troy? was I ever there?

Book Two

[1]

We have had the dream, delirium, trance, ecstasy. We have had Helen in Egypt and Helen in Leuké, l'isle blanche. Where is she now? She had said to Theseus, "I must have time to remember." She had said to Theseus, "teach me to remember . . . teach me not to remember." We feel that there is a balanced perfection in her surroundings, her state of mind, "as light begins — but far, far to show outline through the curtain." This is waking-dream or day-dream.

Helen: Why do I call him my son and Achilles'?
because of an ember, because of a Star?
(was there ever such a brazier?)

because of an old flint
he found in his pouch,
("I thought I had lost that")

because of the armful of dead sticks
he gathered and dried weed
I stooped to scrape from the sand

and fling on the fire? I remember
the crackle of salt-weed,
the sting of salt as I crept nearer

over shale and the white shells;
O, I remember, I remember,
here with the embers glowing,

but fainter, growing dimmer
as light begins — but far, far
to show outline through the curtain,

as of a ladder — an old shutter
with a broken slat? — but the ladder is even,
seven slats and seven —

what do I remember?
we met on a desolate coast,
maybe he is old — adepts are ageless,

and Paris has far to go,
in that he is young, in that he is our son;
yet what have you accomplished,

O, Paris, beautiful enchanter?
you would re-live an old story,
Oedipus and his slain father,

you would re-create Troy
with Helen, not Hecuba for mother;
did I ever stand on the ramparts?

did you ever let fly the dart?
I only remember the shells, whiter than bone,
on the ledge of a desolate beach . . .

2

Yes, Achilles spoke, Paris spoke. Greece and Troy challenged and contradicted each other in her fantasy. She had said to The-seus, "there is a voice within me, listen —" But we do not feel that Achilles and Paris were "a voice within" her. They were dis-parate beings, separate from each other and separate from Helen. How bring them together? But why bring them together? Perhaps it is the very force of opposition that creates the dynamic intensity of "the high-altar, your couch here."

Achilles said, which was the veil,
which was the dream?
truly, Troy had never been

till I came here;
then I encountered or seemed to remember
an old enchantment, an old lover;

it seemed real till he insisted,
she died, died, died,
when the Walls fell;

Helen was never dead,
or is this death here?
Achilles said, a catafalque, a bier,

the high-altar, your couch here;
surely, it was his voice that spoke,
and Paris reviled him,

though I did not see them, or did I?
their words contradict each other,
Theseus would have the answer,

but no, I will not call
until I review all the past
in the new light of a new day.

3

The opposites have been reconciled, actually, in Theseus. "The lyre or the sword? Theseus has both together." Where Theseus is, Athens is. Where Helen is — ? For the first time in our sequence, she is in Sparta. What had she lost? What had she gained? She had lost her childhood or her child, her "Lord's devotion" or the devotion of the conventional majority.

The lyre or the sword?
Theseus has both together,
this is Athens, he said;

this is Athens or was or will be,
but O the ecstasy — familiar fragrance,
late roses, bruised apples,

now I remember, I remember
Paris before Egypt, Paris after;
I remember all that went before,

Sparta; autumn? summer?
the fragrant bough? fruit ripening
on a wall? the ships at anchor?

I had all that, everything,
my Lord's devotion, my child
prattling of a bird-nest,

playing with my work-basket;
the reels rolled to the floor
and she did not stoop to pick up

the scattered spools but stared
with wide eyes in a white face,
at a stranger — and stared at her mother,

a stranger — that was all,
I placed my foot on the last step
of the marble water-stair

and never looked back;
how could I remember all that?
Zeus, our-father was merciful.

4

What had she gained? She had gained "a rhythm as yet un-heard."

What was the charm?
a touch — so a hand
brushes the lyre-strings;

a whisper — a breath
to invite the rose;
a summer touch,

night-wings or vermillion
of the day-butterfly;
was Troy lost for a subtle chord,

a rhythm as yet un-heard,
was it Apollo's snare?
was Apollo passing there?

was a funeral-pyre to be built,
a holocaust of the Greeks,
because of a fluttering veil,

or because Apollo granted a lute-player,
a rhythm as yet unheard,
to challenge the trumpet-note?

[5]

There is no question of Helen's integrity nor even of the old antagonists, "Eros? Eris?" There is a story, a song "the harpers will sing forever." It is a play, a drama — "who set the scene? who lured the players?" The players have no choice in the matter of the already-written drama or script. They are supremely aware of the honour that "all song forever" has conferred upon them. They would play their parts well.

Was Troy lost for a kiss,
or a run of notes on a lyre?
was the lyre-frame stronger

than the bowman's arc,
the chord tauter?
was it a challenge to Death,

to all song forever?
was it a question asked
to which there was no answer?

was it Paris? was it Apollo?
was it a game played over and over,
with numbers or counters?

who set the scene?
who lured the players from home
or imprisoned them in the Walls,

to inspire us with endless,
intricate questioning?
why did they fight at all?

was Helen daemon or goddess?
how did they scale the Walls?
was the iron-horse an ancient symbol

or a new battering-ram?
was Helen another symbol,
a star, a ship or a temple?

how will the story end?
was Paris more skillful than Teucer?
Achilles than Hector?

6

Indeed it was "Apollo's snare." None other.

Was it Apollo's snare
so that poets forever,
should be caught in the maze of the Walls

of a Troy that never fell?
was it a round of Delphic priestesses,
beating on Holy Ground,

a rhythm before the altar,
or the crash of sword upon sword
of the Pyrrhic dancers?

how could the lyre-string fail?
I am called back to the Walls
to find the answer,

to wander as in a maze
(Theseus' Labyrinth),
to explore each turn of the street,

for a way to the ships and the wharves,
to return and sort over and over,
my bracelets, sandals and scarves —

232

but who would stoop to pilfer,
who would steal
these intimate, personal things?

the servants were richer than Helen,
counting the links in a chain,
the pearls on a string,

that the merchants should not cheat
a suspect stranger from Greece,
is she a slave or a queen?

7

So Helen remembers her part in the greatest drama of Greece and of all time. She seems almost to speak by rote, she has grown into her part. But she breaks off, as it were, from the recorded drama to remind us of the unrecorded . . . her first meeting with Achilles, "on the ledge of a desolate beach."

Another shout from the wharves;
I fight my way through the crowd,
but the gates are barred;

are the ramparts free?
I am an enemy in a beleaguered city;
I find my way to the Tower,

to the Tower-stairs,
do I run? do I fly?
what pity for Helen?

Hecuba's lordly son
has been slain by Achilles;
could I join the confusion below,

I would leap from the Walls,
but a sentry snatches my sleeve,
dragging me back — what curse

can equal his curse?
how answer his scorn?
"for this is Hector dead,

was Hector born to be conquered
by harlots and thieves,
stealing a prince's honour?

let Paris retrieve
the fate of Priam's city;
he is next to the king

in the Trojan hierarchy,
but we will have no decadent lover
for king, none sick of a fever,

a Grecian harlot brings
to weaken the fibre,
to melt the sinews of war

in a lascivious seven-year dallying";
was it seven years, was it a day?
I can not remember . . .

I only remember the shells,
whiter than bone,
on the ledge of a desolate beach.

8

*There is only a song now and rhetorical questions that have
been already answered.*

Did the harp-string fail,
or did eternal Justice
tip the scale?

was a fluttering veil
a message, a sign
that the waiting was over?

seven years? they said it was ten;
I stood at the stair-head,
the famous spiral-stair,

and heard their shouting
but I did not care,
for Achilles was dead;

how did they force the gate?
how did they fire the Towers?
that was nothing to me

who had waited the endless years,
was it seven years?
was it a day?

an arrow sped from the door
and Paris swerved, but I was gone
before Paris fell;

did the harp-string fail?
was Aphrodite's power
nothing after all?

Book Three

[1]

Again the veil, the dream, bringing the symbolism of the "flut-
tering veil" of which Helen has just spoken into line with "the
horizon." Achilles' early question, "Helena, which was the dream,
which was the veil of Cytheraea?" is answered, and Helen herself
has answered it, "they were one." They are "the ships assembled
at Aulis," and — a mermaid . . .

> Achilles said, which was the veil,
> which was the dream?
> they were one — on the horizon,
>
> a sail sensed, not seen;
> a bow, a familiar prow,
> a hand on the rudder,
>
> ropes, rope-ladders, the smell of tar,
> I think he remembered them all,
> (when he stooped to gather the sticks),
>
> scattered tackle and gear,
> a wheel, a mast, a dipping sail;
> he struck the flint

and the blaze outlined
the skeleton shapes
of the broken sticks

and caught the inflammable weed
in a sudden flare
and a sputter of salt;

what scent? what wind? what hope
on the ledge of a desolate beach?
what did he remember last, what first?

I think he remembered everything
in an instantaneous flash,
as he straightened after he flung

the last faggots down,
and looked at the stars,
swaying as before the mast,

and looked at Helena,
what spirit, what daemon, what ghost?
a host of spirits crowded around the fire

but I did not see them;
he could have named them all,
had he paused to remember,

but he only saw the ships
assembled at Aulis,
he only remembered his own ship

that would lead them all,
he only saw an image, a wooden image,
a mermaid, Thetis upon the prow.

2

Achilles had been alone, for the women that Theseus had named, and the same names as Paris repeats them, are to Helen as she again recalls them, "no problem any more." For Achilles, there is one love and perhaps for Helen, "his own ship that would lead them all."

How could any woman hope
to achieve Victory
over the Sea? name them,

Briseis, Chryseis, Polyxena; name again
Deidamia, the king's daughter,
he married in Scyros;

did any of them matter?
did they count at all,
or were they mere members of a chorus

in a drama that had but one other player?
in any case, the struggle was over,
as I stood at the stair-head

there was no problem any more,
I did not care who won, who lost,
Achilles was dead;

Zeus had rapt you away, Paris said,
there by the spiral-stair,
yes, Zeus had rapt me away,

but had it happened before
the arrow sped from the door
and I was gone before Paris fell?

3

So we see with the eyes of Helen, "*the swords flash.*" We hear
the "*thunder across the plain.*" We feel and know the dedication
of the "*child of Thetis*" to the Sea. We are hardly surprised that
this "*greatest hero in Greece,*" dismissing as it were, the traditional sacrifice of Iphigenia, should promise "*another white throat
to a goddess.*"

I say there is only one image,
one picture, though the swords flash;
I say there is one treasure,

one desire, as the wheels turn
and the hooves of the stallions
thunder across the plain,

and the plain is dust,
and the battle-field is a heap
of rusty staves and broken chariot-frames

and the rims of the dented shields
and desolation, destruction — for what?
a dream? a towered town?

proud youths for slaves,
a princess or two for lust?
I say there is one image,

and slaves and princesses
and the town itself are nothing
beside a picture, an image, an idol

or eidolon, not much more than a doll,
old, old — for ship-rigging and beam
can be changed, a mast renewed,

a rudder re-set but never the hull;
this is the same, this is my first ship,
this is my own, my belovèd

who will lead the host;
we will sail, we will sail
with or without Iphigenia's death,

for I have promised another
white throat to a goddess,
but not to our lady of Aulis.

4

Helen herself seems almost ready for this sacrifice — at least,
for the immolation of herself before this greatest love of Achilles,
his dedication to "his own ship" and the figurehead, "an idol or
eidolon . . . a mermaid, Thetis upon the prow."

Did her eyes slant in the old way?
was she Greek or Egyptian?
had some Phoenician sailor wrought her?

was she oak-wood or cedar?
had she been cut from an awkward block
of ship-wood at the ship-builders,

and afterwards riveted there,
or had the prow itself been shaped
to her mermaid body,

curved to her mermaid hair?
was there a dash of paint
in the beginning, in the garment-fold,

did the blue afterwards wear away?
did they re-touch her arms, her shoulders?
did anyone touch her ever?

had she other zealot and lover,
or did he alone worship her?
did she wear a girdle of sea-weed

or a painted crown? how often
did her high breasts meet the spray,
how often dive down?

5

So Achilles disguised, deserts "the Trojan plain," and "a far shadow upon the beach . . . he went to the prow of his love, his beloved."

Achilles skulks in his tent,
they said, but it was not true,
Achilles avoids the battle;

we will trick him
and lure him out,
Patroclus shall bear his shield

and lead his men;
so they armed Patroclus
and Patroclus was slain;

where is Achilles?
they sought for him everywhere,
but never thought the unarmed

hostler who tended his steeds,
was Achilles' self,
wrapped in a woolen cloak

with the hood drawn over his head;
he skulks in his tent, they said,
but he was a far shadow upon the beach;

"a spy, an emissary of Troy?"
but he answered the sentinel's threat
with the simple pass-word

of Achilles' Myrmidons,
Helena; so he went to the prow
of his love, his beloved,

feeling her flanks,
tearing loose weed from her stern,
brushing sand from her beams,

not speaking, but praying:
I will re-join the Greeks
and the battle before the gate,

if you promise a swift return,
if you promise new sails for the fleet
and a wind to bear us home,

I am sick of the Trojan plain,
I would rise, I would fall again
in a tempest, a hurricane.

6

*And at that most crucial moment, Achilles directs the Battle that
will prove the turning-point of the war and bring final Victory to
the Greeks. But the "power of the tempest" has been misconstrued,
and the "simple pass-word of Achilles' Myrmidons, Helena"
has been forgotten.*

He was the tempest-self
as he roused the host,
and they said, see Achilles' anger,

his unspeakable grief,
for his friend is dead;
he is thundering over the plain,

where is Hector?
when the heroes meet,
the very world must crash

in the clash of their arms;
so they circled the city-wall
three times, till Hector fell;

was this vengeance?
was this answer to prayer?
so the legend starts,

and Patroclus-Achilles are names
to be conjured together;
but the warriors never saw

a shadow upon the beach,
nor knew the power of the tempest
was roused by another.

7

Was Helen stronger than Achilles even "as the arrows fell"? That could not be, but he recognised in her some power other than her legendary beauty.

He could name Helena,
but the other he could not name;
she was a lure, a light,

an intimate flame, a secret kept
even from his slaves, the elect,
the innermost hierarchy;

only Helena could be named
and she was a public scandal
in any case, a cause of shame

to Agamemnon and Menelaus;
it was not that she was beautiful,
true, she stood on the Walls,

taut and indifferent
as the arrows fell;
it was not that she was beautiful,

there were others,
in spite of the legend,
as gracious, as tall;

it was not that she was beautiful,
but he stared and stared
across the charred wood

and the smouldering flame,
till his eyes cleared
and the smoke drifted away.

[8]

"So she cheated at last." It is not granted human or super-human intelligence and ingenuity to escape the "lure of the sea."

Did her eyes slant in the old way?
was she Greek or Egyptian?
it was not his own ship

but a foreign keel
that had brought him here;
the Old Man who ferried him out,

called it a caravel;
a caravel — what is that?
Phoenician? so she cheated at last,

she, Empress and lure of the sea,
Queen of the Myrmidons,
Regent of heaven and the star-zone;

she had promised him immortality
but she had forgotten to dip the heel
of the infant Achilles

into the bitter water,
Styx, was it?
O careless, unspeakable mother,

O Thetis . . .
so she failed at last,
and worse than failure,

the mockery, after-death,
to stumble across a stretch
of shell and the scattered weed,

to encounter another
whose eyes slant in the old way;
is she Greek or Egyptian?

Book Four

[1]

Helen says, "I am awake, I see things clearly; it is dawn." If the Helen of our first sequence was translated to a transcendental plane, the Amen-temple in Egypt, and the Helen of our second sequence contacted a guide or guardian, near to her in time, Theseus, the hero-king and "Master of Argo," our third Helen having realized "all myth, the one reality," is concerned with the human content of the drama. "I am awake, I see things clearly." Clearly, she realizes the "death" of Achilles and his "ecstasy of desolation, a desire to return to the old thunder and roar of the sea."

So it was nothing, nothing at all,
the loss, the gain; it was nothing,
the victory, the shouting

and Hector slain; it was nothing,
the days of waiting were over;
perhaps his death was bitter,

I do not know; I am awake,
I see things clearly; it is dawn,
the light has changed only a little,

the day will come;
did he speak to me?
he seemed to say, it was nothing,

the arid plain, only the wind,
tearing the canvas loose,
and the tent-pole swaying,

and I lying on my pallet, awake
and hearing the flap of the sail,
the creak of the mast in the mast-hold,

and caring nothing for heat,
nothing for cold,
numb with a memory,

a sort of ecstasy of desolation,
a desire to return to the old
thunder and roar of the sea . . .

waiting to join Hector,
but I can not be slain,
I am immortal, invincible,

son of a Greek king;
did she taunt him then,
the little image,

fearless to plough the sea,
did she laugh to see her son,
entrapped in the armoury

of iron and ruin?
did she come,
his eidolon?

2

*So this third Helen, for the moment, rejects both the transcen-
dental Helen and the intellectual or inspired Helen for this other,
"numb with a memory."*

So it was nothing, nothing at all,
the first words he seemed to speak
in my fever, awake or asleep;

it was nothing, the corridors,
the temple, the temple walls,
the tasks of the star-beasts,

the words I had spoken before
to Theseus, and my prayer;
it was nothing, the Amen-script,

the Writing, the star-space,
the Wheel and the Mystery;
it was all nothing,

and the anger of Paris
was only a breath to fan the flame
of thoughts too deep to remember,

that break through the legend,
the fame of Achilles,
the beauty of Helen,

like fire
through the broken pictures
on a marble-floor.

3

The memory is really that of Achilles but she lives it with him.

It was only then,
when the pictures had melted away,
that I saw him stretched on his pallet,

that I seemed to hear him say,
she failed me, my Daemon, my Goddess;
she had led him astray,

prompting an Old Man to guide her son
to a battered, unwieldly craft;
true, the boat had a mast,

but otherwise, it was a foreign
unseemly thing, with awkward sails —
where are the Thetis-wings?

it was only, when I felt
with him, lying there,
the bitterness of his loss,

that I knew he loved, that I knew
the ecstasy of desire had smitten him,
burnt him; touched with the Phoenix-fire,

the invincible armour
melted him quite away,
till he knew his mother;

but he challenged her, beat her back,
are you Hecate? are you a witch?
a vulture, a hieroglyph?

4

*Helen "had watched as a careful craftsman, the pattern shape."
Indeed, she could never have done this, if she had not had the ardu-
ous, preliminary training or instruction of the Amen-script. She
herself had told us that "you may penetrate every shrine, an initiate, and remain unenlightened at last." Is the last enlightenment
that of the woman Helen? Is it after all, as she had said, "very
simple"?*

As a circlet may break
in the heat of the smelting-fire,
or a plate of armour crack

or a buckler snap
or an axle-tree give way
or a wheel-rim twist awry,

so it seemed to me
that I had watched,
as a careful craftsman,

the pattern shape,
Achilles' history,
that I had seen him like the very scenes

on his famous shield,
outlined with the graver's gold;
true, I had met him, the New Mortal,

baffled and lost,
but I was a phantom Helen
and he was Achilles' ghost.

5

Yes — Helen is awake, she sees the pattern; the "old pictures" are eternal, the ibis, the hawk and the hare are painted in bright primary colours. But superimposed on the hieroglyphs is the "marble and silver" of her Greek thought and fantasy.

Perhaps his death was bitter,
I do not know: I am awake,
the slats of the shutter make

a new pattern, seven and seven,
as the light moves over the wall;
I think I see clearly at last,

the old pictures are really there,
eternal as the painted ibis in Egypt,
the hawk and the hare,

but written in marble and silver,
the spiral-stair, the maze
of the intricate streets,

each turn of the winding
and secret passage-ways
that led to the sea,

my meanderings back and forth,
till I learned by rote
the intimate labyrinth

that I kept in my brain,
going over and over again
the swiftest way to take

through this arched way or that,
patient to re-trace my steps
or swift to dart

past a careless guard at the gate;
O, I knew my way,
O, I knew my ways,

and a sombre scarf
hid Helena's eyes,
but not Helena's passionate speech,

"only a Master Mariner
at the wharves — here is silver,
let me pass."

6

Helen was seeking the "Master Mariner"; she does not find him, though her preliminary search leads finally to the "Master of Argo."

Is this a dream
or was a lover waiting there?
I only know that I climbed

up a ladder or wooden stair,
I only know that I slipped
on the floating weed

near the edge — was it Simois' river?
was it the sea?
it was a harbour, a bay or estuary;

I only know that I lay
on the salt grass and my hands
tore at the bitter stems

that cut me like adders' tongues;
it was dark, I had not the power
to leap from the platform or wharf;

O, it was dark
so I lost my lover;
I slid on a broken rung

and my hand instinctively caught
at the skeleton-frame of the ladder
and I had not the strength to drown.

No, Helen can not escape from Troy through physical death.
Now she is glad of her return, she is "happy to see the dawn."
She was saved for this, La Mort, L'Amour.

Whom did I seek?
whom did I think waited me there?
but I was not wanted,

no Old Man would ferry me out
to a craft, however old, however worn
and battered in foreign seas,

no one wanted me, Helena;
I am happy to see the dawn,
to remember the ladder

and the broken slat or rung
I forgot before;
remembering desolation, I remember

that other stretch of sea-weed
and the fire; I remember
the hands that ringed my throat

and no moment's doubt,
this is Love, this is Death,
this is my last Lover.

*Indeed, the enchantment, the magic, at the time and equally in
retrospect, is over-powering. It could not have been endured but
"for her." It was to Thetis that Helen prayed, on her first encounter with Achilles. Now the "eternal moment" returns and
"we stare and stare over the smouldering embers."*

For her, it is clear,
(are you near, are you far),
for her, we are One,

not for each other,
for we stare and stare
over the smouldering embers,

and it is undecided yet,
whether Achilles turn and tear
the Circe, the enchantress,

the Hecate by the witches fire,
whether he snarl,
turned lion or panther

or another, wolf or bear;
they all seem to prowl around her
while she waits

and the circle grows smaller;
will what she invoked
destroy her?

nearer, nearer —
till I felt the touch
of his fingers' remorseless steel . . .

for I have promised another
white throat to a goddess,
but not to our lady of Aulis.

Book Five

[1]

*So they will always be centralized by a moment, "undecided
yet." Though La Mort, L'Amour will merge in the final illu-
mination, there is this preliminary tension that can be symbolized
by the "circle of god-like beasts." The great "frieze, the Zodiac
hieroglyph" comes to life with the magnetic intensity of these two.
Forever, there is "the pad of paws on the sand . . . "*

Did he fear her more
than I could ever fear
the pad of paws on the sand,

the glare of eyes in the fire,
the lion or the crouching panther?
it almost seemed they were there,

the circle of god-like beasts,
familiars of Egypt;
would they turn and rend each other,

or form a frieze,
the Zodiac hieroglyph,
on a temple wall?

they are there forever, quiet
or slow to move
like their Guardians in heaven;

I might have counted them, twelve,
the outline of hero and beast,
or I might have counted seven

and seven, like the bars of light
that have slowly climbed up the wall;
I might have numbered them over,

I might have implored or invoked
the planets of the day,
the planets of the night.

2

Though there is the intense, almost unbearable excitement in this circle of "god-like beasts," Helen does not invoke the power of lion or panther, wolf or bear. Undoubtedly, she is at one with them. She loves them, certainly, nor does she dismiss them. She is not afraid of them but she feels that Achilles is afraid of something. That fear creates the tension that he expresses in his attack, "are you Hecate? are you a witch?" Maybe. If so, she had already proved the invincibility of the "lure of the sea, Queen of Myrmidons, Regent of heaven and the star-zone." So again, Helen "cried to one Daemon only, the goddess I knew from his eyes, was his mother, the sea-enchantment."

But I did not entreat the twelve
nor the seven and the seven,
I cried to one Daemon only,

the goddess I knew from his eyes,
was his mother, the sea-enchantment;
did she harbour them there,

in the caves of the Mysteries,
when they wheeled and fell from heaven?
was it Thetis who herded the flock,

the two and the two, begotten
of light and of dark?
was it Thetis who lured him here,

in a battered ship with a mast
that measured the sky-space
and the space beneath the sky,

in the infinite depth of the sea
that she rules with the arc of heaven,
with day and night equally?

was it fate, was it destiny
that brought us together?
would we blaze out like a meteor?

would the blazing ember
sputter and fail and fall
or burn forever?

3

We have seen that Thetis, like Proteus, takes many forms. Nor will she neglect "the worshippers from the caves." To each adept of darkness, it seems, she appoints a companion "from the circles of heaven." Helen had asked of "the lion and the crouching panther," if they would "turn and rend each other." No. So, the assembled "host of spirits" form "the whole arc . . . the circle complete."

Had it happened before?
it could not happen again,
not one, not the whole arc,

not the circle complete,
enclosing the day and the night;
under and through the sea

she had sought them out,
she had gathered the worshippers
from the caves, and the host of light

from the circles of heaven,
two and two, brothers and sons,
like my own twins, the Dioscuri;

a host of spirits crowded around the fire,
but I did not see them;
he could have named them all,

had he paused to remember,
but he was seared with an agony,
the question that has no answer.

[4]

There is a word. Helen has spoken it. "How did she know the word?" It may not seem a matter of great importance that in their first encounter, she "dared speak the name that made that of the goddess fade," but apparently, "a whisper, a breath" of which Helen, it seems, was unaware, had alarmed Achilles ("O child of Thetis"), provoked his attack and projected the first of the series or circle of the ever-recurring "eternal moment."

How did she know the word,
the one word that would turn and bind
and blind him to any other?

he could name Helena
but the other he could not name;
she spoke of the goddess Isis,

and he answered her "Isis,"
but how did she know that her Thetis
(that followed immediately after

he repeated after her, "Isis"),
would brand on his forehead
that name, that the name

and the flame and the fire
would weld him to her
who spoke it, who thought it,

who stared through the fire,
who stood as if to withstand
the onslaught of fury and battle,

who stood unwavering but made
as if to dive down, unbroken,
undefeated in the tempest roar

and thunder, inviting mountains
of snow-clad foam-tipped
green walls of sea-water

to rise like ramparts about her,
walls to protect yet walls to dive under,
dive through and dive over;

how dared she speak the name
that made that of the goddess fade
or stiffen in painted folds

in a niche above an altar;
"pray, pray your vulture, your Isis,"
he seemed to say;

but there is one secret,
unpronounceable name,
a whisper, a breath,

two syllables, yes, like the Isis-name,
but broken, not quite the same,
breathed differently,

or spoken as only one could speak,
stretched on a pallet,
numb with a memory,

or as a sleepless child,
crouched in the leaves
of Chiron's cave.

5

What is this "simple magic" of a "ring of no worth, a broken oar" that finds more favour in the eyes of the "Regent of heaven" than the priceless treasure "from the uttermost seas"?

How did she know the name?
true, the world knew her,
she is carved on the harbour walls,

she is found on the lintel or set
in a niche under the eaves,
like a bird in a bird-nest,

a man will barter or filch
anything for the grains
left in an emptied sack

of incense-sticks or wait
to barter or share with another
scattered shreds of the sandal-bark,

a man will wait hours on the wharf
for some chance unexpected thing,
the simple magic coming

from something lost or left over,
or spilled like the ash-of-myrrh
on the Paphos-temple floor,

which a simple servant (no priestess)
sweeps up to bring to another;
Oh, yes, the world knows her name,

the richer for poorer worshippers,
for meaner offerings,
a filigree ring of no worth,

a broken oar, a snapped anchor-chain;
why did they bring her these,
when the whole world saw

sea-chests from the uttermost seas,
empty their priceless treasure
on the Paphos-altar?

6

Perhaps it can not be defined. It is a "secret treasure" but Helen implies, as she counts "the seven and seven slats of the ladder or the bars of light on the wall," that it could only be judged or assessed if "God would let me lie here forever."

It was a treasure beyond a treasure
he gave her, no buckle
detached from his gear,

a trophy to prove to others,
Achilles had loved her;
no strip of leather,

stained with the heat of battle,
such as Briseis might show
as proof to another,

or Chryseis display forever,
as a conqueror's favour;
what did he give her?

it was nothing, nothing at all,
and was this his anger,
that something forgotten or lost,

like the flint in his pouch
("I thought I had lost that"),
was taken from him,

and he only remembered it,
remembered and wanted it back,
when it was gone?

that I only remembered and treasured
the gift I forced from him,
long after — is it seven years,

is it a day? if only God
would let me lie here forever,
I could assess, weigh and value

the secret treasure, as I count
the seven and the seven slats of the ladder
or the bars of light on the wall.

7

Chiron, the Centaur had trained most of the Greek heroes, out-standing among them, Achilles. So Helen recalls the scene of his boyhood and his childhood's secret idol, the first Thetis-eidolon.

He could thunder, entreat and command,
and she would obey — that was natural,
she was his mother;

he could whisper, enchant and pray
with flute-note or whistle bird-note
on the reed-pipe that Chiron had made;

but the Centaur had not wrought nor charmed
nor conjured this thing
that worked magic, always answering,

always granting his wish or whim;
he hid it in moss, in straw,
in a hole in the cave-wall

or in the tree by the cave-door,
and stone by fitted stone,
he built her an altar,

it was far on the hill-crest
but the other was always near,
and the Centaur being a god,

did not help him,
nor try to find
what filled the eyes of the child

with terrible fire —
fire of battle?
fire of desire?

8

But with "the lure of war," the hero forgot "the magic of little things," and his mother's "simple wish that he learn to rule a kingdom," until in the end, "he paused to remember, but he was seared with an agony, the question that has no answer."

He knew the trick, the magic
of little things, how the reapers
brought his mother the gleanings

and not the sheaves,
but he had been lured from Scyros,
where she hid her son,

entreating the king to instruct him,
as the Centaur Chiron had done,
in the laws and the arts of peace;

for none could reach the youth
in the race, he so far out-paced
the others, he seemed to run alone,

and none could teach him anything
of the ways of the bird or the beast,
and none dared draw the bow

286

where the young Achilles stood;
his were Chiron's arrows;
hers was a simple wish

that he learn to rule a kingdom,
but he had forgotten Scyros,
forgotten his vows of allegiance

to the king, forgotten his marriage-vows
to the king's daughter;
he had followed the lure of war,

and there was never a braver,
a better among the heroes,
but he stared and stared

through the smoke and the glowing embers,
and wondered why he forgot
and why he just now remembered.

Book Six

[1]

There is the ultimate experience, La Mort, L'Amour. *But Helen "in the new light of a new day," fully realizes the price of that ultimate. Is the price too great? "The numberless tender kisses, the soft caresses" have no part in the epic. But there is a miraculous birth. The promised* Euphorion *is not one child but two. It is "the child in Chiron's cave" and the "frail maiden," stolen by Theseus from Sparta.*

I only saw him from the ramparts
and on the desolate beach,
and we talked apart in the temple;

true, we followed a track in the sand
though we spoke but little,
and the absolute, final spark,

the ember, the Star had no personal,
intimate fervour; was it desire?
it was Love, it was Death,

but what followed before, what after?
a thousand-thousand days,
as many mysterious nights,

and multiplied to infinity,
the million personal things,
things remembered, forgotten,

remembered again, assembled
and re-assembled in different order
as thoughts and emotions,

the sun and the seasons changed,
and as the flower-leaves that drift
from a tree were the numberless

tender kisses, the soft caresses,
given and received; none of these
came into the story,

it was epic, heroic and it was far
from a basket a child upset
and the spools that rolled to the floor;

and if I think of a child of Achilles,
it is not Pyrrhus, his son,
they called Neoptolemus,

nor any of all the host that claimed as father,
the Myrmidon's Lord and Leader,
but the child in Chiron's cave;

and if I remember a child that stared
at a stranger and the child's name is Hermione,
it is not Hermione

I would stoop and shelter,
remembering the touch on my shoulder,
the enchanter's power.

2

Helen had recalled "the fragrant bough," when she thought of
her childhood in Sparta. Now she thinks of "a sorcery even more
potent," that of the child Achilles. A tree holds the secret "that
Thetis' child hid away."

Paris is beautiful enchantment
and enchantment lives
in the tree he called *Dendritis*,

while another tree,
the tree before Chiron's door,
holds another secret,

a sorcery even more potent,
a wooden doll
that Thetis' child hid away;

O mysterious treasure,
O idol, O eidolon,
with wings folded about her,

her hands are clasped as in prayer,
in the garment-fold;
is she carved of red-cedar?

only a child could follow
the living grain of the tree,
as if sap were rising within her,

only a child or a master-hand
could fit a crown or a cap
from the rose-vein of the wood;

he set her upon a plinth
like the curved prow of a ship,
and perhaps the tree is a ship

and he sails away, but he forgot her,
the charm, the eidolon,
when his own mother came,

and he forgot his mother
when the heroes mocked
at the half-god hidden in Scyros.

3

But what is "the living grain of the tree" and "the rose-vein of the wood" to "one brandished spear that enflames a thousand others"?

Did she rise and fall
like the ebb and flow of the sea?
not she, her power was measureless,

she could not fail,
but could she understand?
could a woman ever

know what the heroes felt,
what spurred them to war and battle,
what fire charged them with fever?

like the lightning-flash
was the flash of their metal,
the spark from their sword and steel;

O spear of light,
O torch of one brandished spear
that enflames a thousand others,

O light reflected from polished buckler
and shield, a mirror to show the dead,
we may not look upon,

lest we pause and waver
and question the chances of war;
O glory of Pallas,

O Gorgon-head,
turn us not to stone, let us live to strike
merciless strokes for the Flower

that is Greece,
her hearth-stone and altar;
so the warriors spoke,

so the warriors lured him out;
what can a woman know
of man's passion and birthright?

4

True, he forgot her and that is where her power lay. Was not his own mother more desirable than the "wooden doll" he had made to represent her? The prophecy of Achilles' fame could only be fulfilled if he died in battle. So "his own mother came" and Thetis "hid him in Scyros." But the heroes found him and "mocked," and that was the end of Thetis' plan for her son's inheritance of the island-kingdom. But "a sorcery even more potent" was to claim him in the end.

Paris said she was poor,
when she walked (as he said I walked)
to the door; they were rich

in their battle array,
their gold and their silver;
true, they emptied their sea-chests

and coffers upon the Paphian's altar,
but there was another Love,
another Love's mother,

secret, hidden away under Achilles' armour;
he lost his arms, his famous shield,
when Patroclus fell, but Thetis

entreated Hephaestus to forge again,
another helmet and greaves
with sword and sword-belt and buckler,

but she left him defenceless;
he could name the heroes who lived,
who died in a just defence

of a cause, he was blameless
like all the rest,
like Agamemnon and Menelaus;

she fought for the Greeks, they said,
Achilles' mother, but Thetis mourned
like Hecuba, for Hector dead.

5

What was that sorcery or magic? It can only be defined by the most abstruse hieroglyphs or the most simple memories. All between, Helen seems to tell us is "nothing, nothing at all." But there is something between. There is the old problem, "how reconcile Trojan and Greek?" In the beginning of this sequence, the voices of Achilles and Paris seemed to argue, unreconciled. Helen woke to struggle with the problem, in the human dimension, "my mind goes on, spinning the infinite thread." Helen is "awake, no trance." In a trance, "on the gold-burning sands of Egypt," she may have solved the problem. And Theseus, wholly intellectual and inspirational, resolved it with his "all myth, the one reality dwells here." But Helen says, "did I challenge the Fates when I said to Theseus, 'the Wheel is still'?"

Was it nothing, nothing at all,
I asked when I heard Paris say,
"call on Thetis, the sea-mother";

but why was it Paris who spoke?
and why did I call him back?
what formula did I plot,

like an old enchanter?
how reconcile Trojan and Greek?
my mind goes over the problem,

297

round and round like the chariot-wheel;
did I challenge the Fates
when I said to Theseus,

"the Wheel is still"?
my mind goes on,
spinning the infinite thread;

surely, I crossed the threshold,
I passed through the temple-gate,
I crossed a frontier and stepped

on the gold-burning sands of Egypt;
then why do I lie here and wonder,
and try to unravel the tangle

that no man can ever un-knot?
I was quiet, I slept, then a fever
ravaged my heart and my thought;

who after all, is Paris?
why did he say, "call on Thetis"?
they are centuries, worlds apart.

6

*It is not so simple. Helen seems to wish to return to an easier
"formula." But the "sea-mother," whether we call her Thetis,
Isis or Aphrodite, mourns "for Hector dead." On our first meeting
with Helen, in the Amen-temple, she recalls "the glory and the
beauty of the ships." These were Greek ships. In this last phase
or mood, it seems inevitable and perhaps wholly human for Helen
to turn on her Trojan lover,* "what can Paris know of the
sea?"

What can Paris know of the sea,
except for the lure and delight
of the sheltered harbours and bays?

what can Paris know of the sea?
he crossed to Sparta, you say,
but the Paphian lightened his craft

and stilled the waves;
what can Paris know of the sea
that Thetis should champion him?

how dared he say to me,
"call on Thetis, the sea-mother"?
I tremble, I feel the same

anger and sudden terror,
that I sensed Achilles felt,
when I named his mother;

true, the world knows her name,
the world may bring her
marble to build her walls,

and ships for her harbours;
but her wings are folded about her
and her wings only un-furl

at the cry of the New Mortal,
or the child's pitiful call;
what had Paris to give her?

7

Helen returns to the two voices and again, almost grudgingly it seems, contrasts them. She had not known Paris in Egypt, but she had said, "Paris is beautiful enchantment," and at the last, "Paris before Egypt, Paris after, is Eros." L'Amour? Yet there is no refutation of her final decision or choice, "there is no before and no after, there is one finite moment." Is this the "eternal moment" of her constant preoccupation, La Mort?

Is it death to stay in Egypt?
is it death to stay here,
in a trance, following a dream?

Achilles said, a catafalque, a bier,
Paris said, call on Thetis;
what had Paris to give her?

it lies at her feet
with torn nets and the spears,
the fishing-nets and the chariot-staves,

mixed offerings of rich and poor,
of peace and of war;
I see the pitiful heap of little things,

the mountain of monstrous gear,
then both vanish, there is nothing,
nothing at all, a single arrow;

what had Paris to give her, or Eros?
for even the aim of Achilles
was not so sure, his bow so taut,

and even the arrow of Chiron
might sometime fail the mark,
but this one, never.

8

*One greater than Helen must answer, though perhaps we do
not wholly understand the significance of the Message.*

Paris before Egypt, Paris after,
is Eros, even as Thetis,
the sea-mother, is Paphos;

so the dart of Love
is the dart of Death,
and the secret is no secret;

the simple path
refutes at last
the threat of the Labyrinth,

the Sphinx is seen,
the Beast is slain
and the Phoenix-nest

reveals the innermost
key or the clue to the rest
of the mystery;

there is no before and no after,
there is one finite moment
that no infinite joy can disperse

or thought of past happiness
tempt from or dissipate;
now I know the best and the worst;

the seasons revolve around
a pause in the infinite rhythm
of the heart and of heaven.

Eidolon

But what could Paris know of the sea,
its beat and long reverberation,
its booming and delicate echo,

its ripple that spells a charm
on the sand, the rock-lichen,
the sea-moss, the sand,

and again and again, the sand;
what does Paris know of the hill and hollow
of billows, the sea-road?

what could he know of the ships
from his Idaean home,
the crash and spray of the foam,

the wind, the shoal, the broken shale,
the infinite loneliness
when one is never alone?

only Achilles could break his heart
and the world for a token,
a memory forgotten.

New Directions Paperbooks

Vladimir Nabokov, *Nikolai Gogol.* NDP78.
P. Neruda, *The Captain's Verses.*† NDP345.
Residence on Earth.† NDP340.
New Directions 17. (Anthology) NDP103.
New Directions 18. (Anthology) NDP163.
New Directions 19. (Anthology) NDP214.
New Directions 20. (Anthology) NDP248.
New Directions 21. (Anthology) NDP277.
New Directions 22. (Anthology) NDP291.
New Directions 23. (Anthology) NDP315.
New Directions 24. (Anthology) NDP332.
New Directions 25. (Anthology) NDP339.
New Directions 26. (Anthology) NDP353.
New Directions 27. (Anthology) NDP359.
New Directions 28. (Anthology) NDP371.
New Directions 29. (Anthology) NDP378.
Charles Olson, *Selected Writings.* NDP231.
George Oppen, *The Materials.* NDP122.
Of Being Numerous. NDP245.
This In Which. NDP201.
Wilfred Owen, *Collected Poems.* NDP210.
Nicanor Parra, *Emergency Poems.*† NDP333.
Poems and Antipoems.† NDP242.
Boris Pasternak, *Safe Conduct.* NDP77.
Kenneth Patchen, *Aflame and Afun of
Walking Faces.* NDP292.
Because It Is. NDP83.
But Even So. NDP265.
Collected Poems. NDP284.
Doubleheader. NDP211.
Hallelujah Anyway. NDP219.
In Quest of Candlelighters. NDP334.
The Journal of Albion Moonlight. NDP99.
Memoirs of a Shy Pornographer. NDP205.
Selected Poems. NDP160.
Sleepers Awake. NDP286.
Wonderings. NDP320.
Octavio Paz, *Configurations.*† NDP303.
Early Poems.† NDP354.
Plays for a New Theater. (Anth.) NDP216.
Ezra Pound, *ABC of Reading.* NDP89.
Classic Noh Theatre of Japan. NDP79.
The Confucian Odes. NDP81.
Confucius. NDP285.
Confucius to Cummings. (Anth.) NDP126.
Gaudier-Brzeska. NDP372.
Guide to Kulchur. NDP257.
Literary Essays. NDP250.
Love Poems of Ancient Egypt. NDP178.
Pound/Joyce. NDP296.
Selected Cantos. NDP304.
Selected Letters 1907-1941. NDP317.
Selected Poems. NDP66.
The Spirit of Romance. NDP266.
Translations.† (Enlarged Edition) NDP145.
Omar Pound, *Arabic and Persian Poems.*
NDP305.
James Purdy, *Children Is All.* NDP327.
Raymond Queneau, *The Bark Tree.* NDP314.
The Flight of Icarus. NDP358.
M. Randall, *Part of the Solution.* NDP350.
John Crowe Ransom, *Beating the Bushes.*
NDP324.
Raja Rao, *Kanthapura.* NDP224.
Herbert Read, *The Green Child.* NDP208.
P. Reverdy, *Selected Poems.*† NDP346.
Kenneth Rexroth, *Assays.* NDP113.
An Autobiographical Novel. NDP281.
Beyond the Mountains. NDP384.
Bird in the Bush. NDP80.
Collected Longer Poems. NDP309.
Collected Shorter Poems. NDP243.
Love and the Turning Year. NDP308.
New Poems. NDP383.

100 Poems from the Chinese. NDP192.
100 Poems from the Japanese.† NDP147.
Arthur Rimbaud, *Illuminations.*† NDP56.
Season in Hell & Drunken Boat.† NDP97.
Selden Rodman, *Tongues of Fallen Angels.*
NDP373.
Jerome Rothenberg, *Poland/1931.* NDP379.
Saikaku Ihara, *The Life of an Amorous
Woman.* NDP270.
St. John of the Cross, *Poems.*† NDP341.
Jean-Paul Sartre, *Baudelaire.* NDP233.
Nausea. NDP82.
The Wall (Intimacy). NDP272.
Delmore Schwartz, *Selected Poems.* NDP241.
Stevie Smith, *Selected Poems.* NDP159.
Gary Snyder, *The Back Country.* NDP249.
Earth House Hold. NDP267.
Regarding Wave. NDP306.
Turtle Island. NDP381.
Gilbert Sorrentino, *Splendide-Hôtel.* NDP364.
Enid Starkie, *Arthur Rimbaud.* NDP254.
Stendhal, *Lucien Leuwen.*
Book II: *The Telegraph.* NDP108.
Jules Supervielle, *Selected Writings.*† NDP209.
W. Sutton, *American Free Verse.* NDP351.
Dylan Thomas, *Adventures in the Skin Trade.*
NDP183.
A Child's Christmas in Wales. NDP181.
Collected Poems 1934-1952. NDP316.
The Doctor and the Devils. NDP297.
Portrait of the Artist as a Young Dog.
NDP51.
Quite Early One Morning. NDP90.
Under Milk Wood. NDP73.
Lionel Trilling, *E. M. Forster.* NDP189.
Martin Turnell, *Art of French Fiction.* NDP251.
Baudelaire. NDP336.
Paul Valéry, *Selected Writings.*† NDP184.
Elio Vittorini, *A Vittorini Omnibus.* NDP366.
Women of Messina. NDP365.
Vernon Watkins, *Selected Poems.* NDP221.
Nathanael West, *Miss Lonelyhearts &
Day of the Locust.* NDP125.
George F. Whicher, tr.,
The Goliard Poets.† NDP206.
J. Willett, *Theatre of Bertolt Brecht.* NDP244.
J. Williams, *An Ear in Bartram's Tree.* NDP335.
Tennessee Williams, *Camino Real.* NDP301.
Dragon Country. NDP287.
Eight Mortal Ladies Possessed. NDP374.
The Glass Menagerie. NDP218.
Hard Candy. NDP225.
In the Winter of Cities. NDP154.
One Arm & Other Stories. NDP237.
Out Cry. NDP367.
The Roman Spring of Mrs. Stone. NDP271.
Small Craft Warnings. NDP348.
27 Wagons Full of Cotton. NDP217.
William Carlos Williams,
The Autobiography. NDP223.
The Build-up. NDP259.
The Farmers' Daughters. NDP106.
Imaginations. NDP329.
In the American Grain. NDP53.
In the Money. NDP240.
Many Loves. NDP191.
Paterson. Complete. NDP152.
Pictures from Brueghel. NDP118.
The Selected Essays. NDP273.
Selected Poems. NDP131.
A Voyage to Pagany. NDP307.
White Mule. NDP226.
W. C. Williams Reader. NDP282.
Yvor Winters,
Edwin Arlington Robinson. NDP326.

Complete descriptive catalog available free on request from
New Directions, 333 Sixth Avenue, New York 10014.   † Bilingual.